All the Classroom Is a Stage:
The Creative Classroom Environment

Pergamon Titles of Related Interest

Ford — Health Education: A Source Book for Teaching

Hillner — Psychology of Learning: A Conceptual Analysis

O'Leary & O'Leary — Classroom Management: The Successful Use of Behavior Modification (Second Edition)

Ritter — Educreation: Education for Creation, Growth and Change (Second Edition)

All the Classroom Is a Stage: The Creative Classroom Environment

Shirley F. Heck
Jon P. Cobes

Pictorial Illustrations
Jon Cobes

Draftsman of Technical Illustrations
James Thorpe

Pergamon Press

NEW YORK • OXFORD • TORONTO • SYDNEY • FRANKFURT • PARIS

Pergamon Press Offices:

U.S.A.   Pergamon Press Inc., Maxwell House, Fairview Park,
                       Elmsford, New York 10523, U.S.A.

U.K.   Pergamon Press Ltd., Headington Hill Hall,
                       Oxford OX3 0BW, England

CANADA   Pergamon of Canada, Ltd., 75 The East Mall,
                       Toronto, Ontario M8Z 5W3, Canada

AUSTRALIA   Pergamon Press (Aust) Pty. Ltd., P O Box 544,
                       Potts Point, NSW 2011, Australia

FRANCE   Pergamon Press SARL, 24 rue des Ecoles,
                       75240 Paris, Cedex 05, France

FEDERAL REPUBLIC   Pergamon Press GmbH, 6242 Kronberg/Taunus,
OF GERMANY   Pferdstrasse 1, Federal Republic of Germany

Library of Congress Cataloging in Publication Data

Heck, Shirley F
    All the classroom is a stage.

    Includes bibliographies.
    1. Education, Elementary--Curriculum. 2. Creative
thinking (Education)   I. Cobes, Jon P., 1932-
II. Title.
LB1570.H39   372.1'9   78-7600
ISBN 0-08-022248-X
ISBN 0-08-022247-1 pbk.

Printed in the United States of America

Contents

List of Figures

Figure

* Names of illustrators are in parentheses

ix

Foreword

Much of the history of teacher education and the performance of teachers in school classrooms has been highly influenced by "teaching as one has been taught." While this continues too often to be the pattern of teacher behavior, in recent years teacher education and the instructional approaches of teachers in classrooms have begun to focus on learning environments that encourage student self-direction and increased learning. This book provides the interdisciplinary framework for student involvement in the learning process through a creative classroom environment.

Professor Heck is uniquely qualified to provide a theoretical base and practical implementation of the "kernel design." She has been a teacher and principal in an open-classroom elementary school. She completed her doctoral studies at The University of Wisconsin, where she was involved in research on individually guided education which is the foundation for the instructional approach represented in this book. She was a key member of the team which designed the fully field-based elementary teacher education program for The Ohio State University at Mansfield.

Her coauthor, Dr. Cobes, has an unusually rich background in theater and library science. He brings to this book practical and easily applied procedures for building simple classroom environments which grow out of his experience in designing and building theater sets.

In short, this book presents creative strategies for teachers to change classroom environments to provide better options for self-directed learning. This book is for a new generation of teachers and teacher educators, those who have experienced the excitement of student self-learning and who wish to find more strategies for encouraging this process.

James B. Heck
Professor of Education, Dean and
Director of The Ohio State
University at Mansfield

Introduction

This book presents an approach to designing the classroom as a stage. The technique, called the kernel design, uses a simplified representation or stage-set design that conveys an awareness of the time, space, or era being studied. Like the scenery which supports the actor in his efforts on the stage, the kernel design provides a creative classroom setting in which the child may research and role-play many of his learning experiences.

Unlike a professional stage-set designer, the teacher need not possess any particular artistic talents. This approach has been used successfully by freshmen education students enrolled in an early field-experience course, by student teachers, and by in-service teachers enrolled in graduate courses. After several quarters of experimenting with the kernel design idea in actual classroom settings, a philosophy and methodology began to emerge. This book, therefore, actually represents the cumulative efforts of university faculty, preservice and in-service teachers, and the grade-school children who reacted so enthusiastically and positively to the integrated learning experience. The enthusiasm of both teachers and students has stimulated the authors to share this approach with other educators who believe that "learning, living, and becoming are continuous and should be integratively related" (Zirbes 1959, p. 76).

This book provides a practical technique whereby many of the emerging principles of the open, informal classroom, individually guided education, and interdisciplinary approaches to teaching can be implemented. The kernel design idea provides many opportunities for a growing, responsible independence through which each child gradually accepts more responsibility for his own education.

The regular social studies curriculum adopted by the school system serves as a core for the development of an atmosphere in which role-playing and researching are encouraged and stimulated. An important premise is that the theater or drama as a literary form is not always necessary for a creative learning situation. Rather, life itself may provide the script. Thus the emphasis of this text on the social studies curriculum. In playing real-world roles in a simplistic but recognizable setting, the child may progressively deal with real-world arithmetic, science, and history; he must read and, in the process of actually contributing to the completed kernel design, he will paint, cut, paste, measure, dance, and sing.   All aspects of the elementary curriculum may be integrated, and the pupil actually lives the learning process.

Children, especially during the first six to eight years of their lives, are egoists with most of the typical adult needs such as success and love. These are, however, stronger and more immediate needs at this age level. Basically, the child's raison d'etre is to become adult; much of his early life is simply a rehearsal for his "real life." The child begins his life and his learning efforts as something of an expert at imitation and role-playing. Often, all he lacks is the script. Our primary effort has been to design a way to make all of learning a truly creative effort, emphasizing the natural dramatic flair of the child as a tool to promote learning and remembering.

Our current technological civilization tends to suppress creativity and interferes, in fact, with the natural need for creative endeavor. When, in the past, survival consumed much of our time and strength, art and leisure to enjoy it was a precious reward. All too often today, the reward has become a way of life; television makes of us professional spectators, experiencing only vicariously the difficulties of survival in a hostile environment. It is interesting to debate whether television broadens or restricts our horizons, whether such obviously contrived situations as are called "dramatic" have any relationship at all to life. Something is missing when a child's view of his community is expressed as a resume of any one of several currently popular television sitcoms. Role-playing in the classroom, not as a substitute for reading or writing, but as a stimulus for research, can once again make the child's creative imagination an important part of growing toward adulthood.

The creative imagination is a private thing. How many teachers have attempted to grade or evaluate creativity and, eventually admitted the task to be impossible! Creative dramatics is a group experience, a sharing, a cooperating effort in which each child is given the scope to express himself freely as he plays and works with others. The kernel design concept differs from true creative dramatics only in that there is a script of sorts. The social studies curriculum adopted by the local school system is the scenario upon which the drama is built and enjoyed, and improvisation is based on newly learned facts.

This book is a text to aid the teacher in integrating the often-diffused elements of classroom decor and activities with the lesson plan for social studies. It emphasizes pupil research and creative effort in the production of a classroom-stage environment that interrelates learning in all curricula. The creative teacher, given a minimum of guidance, can manipulate the classroom environment using free or inexpensive materials to create an acceptable illusion of time and/or place. For example, a two-dimensional cardboard tipi, paper headbands, and feathers are all that are required to begin a unit on the American Indian. As children are encouraged to share, create, and read about various aspects of the many Indian communities, the classroom environment will gradually reflect a re-creation of that community. Child-produced murals, cardboard cutouts of plains, animals and scenes, Indian crafts and implements, science experiments based upon Indian knowledge, plants, and foodstuffs will gradually take the place of the unrelated bulletin board displays and interest centers we so often find in classrooms. If, instead of being an accidental collection process, the entire classroom is thought of as a stage, the completed, shared design effort will be an illusion of the entire community being studied, and the process involved will be learn, live, recall, and use.

REFERENCE

Zirbes, L. Spurs to creative teaching. New York: G.P. Putnam's Sons, 1959.

Acknowledgements

The completion of this book is a tribute to the encouragement and support of many professional and personal acquaintances.   Special appreciation is extended to the following people:

. . . Dr. James B. Heck, Director of The Ohio State University Mansfield Campus, for his continuous encouragement to forge ahead with creative teaching techniques.

. . . Dr. Richard L. Wink, Associate Director of The Ohio State University Mansfield Campus for his editorial assistance and his interest and support in promoting excellence in teaching through scholarship and writing.

. . . Richard L. Kohler, Administrative Coordinator of Discovery School, Mansfield, Ohio - for his contribution to Chapter 13, as well as his professional and personal acquaintance.

. . . All the preservice and in-service teachers enrolled at The Ohio State University Mansfield Campus who accepted the challenge of experimenting with the kernel design approach and to the elementary school children who responded so enthusiastically.

. . . Linda Linn, not only as the expert typist of the manuscript, but as an interested friend.

. . . James Thorpe, for his assistance in drafting many of the more technical illustrations we have created.

. . . We also thank the publisher for use of Figure 3 in Chapter 7. Acknowledgement is to Sir Christopher Wren, St. Paul's (detail of West Front) from John Summerson; ARCHITECTURE IN BRITAIN 1530-1830 (Pelican History of Art, 5th edition, 1969), p. 133. Reprinted by Permission of Penguin Books, Ltd.

1 The Creative Classroom Environment: A Kernel Design Approach

All the world's a stage and all the men and women merely players. They have their exits and their entrances. And one man in his time plays many parts. . . .

> Shakespeare,
> As You Like It

The creative classroom also can be conceived as a stage and the students as its players. This book presents an approach to designing the classroom as a stage so that learning experiences and situations may become life-related and purposeful. The ideas offered help to bridge the gap between the world of the adult and the child's play world through the interplay of carefully planned child-centered lessons, creative classroom environments, and various levels of purely creative activity. To a certain degree the curriculum becomes what Frazier (1976) refers to as "a product of active learning and interactive teaching rather than a curriculum of prestructured content, in which both learning and teaching are intended to be largely passive in character" (p. 272).

To the seven-year-old, even the community in which he lives may be a remote, complex, and dimly understood place of adult problems and standards. The teacher's problem is to humanize the materials of history and communities, to remove the "patina of public monument" from people and places and make them not only meaningful but useful. Ward (1950) offers theater as the medium of representing the world and humanity as it moves through interesting vital epochs and periods of time. Similarly, the authors of this book offer the idea of establishing the classroom as a stage as one solution to the problem of humanizing the materials of history and community. This can be achieved by a technique which the authors call a kernel design.

The kernel design, often made out of large pieces of cardboard, is a simplistic representation or a skeletal construct that conveys an awareness of the time, era, space, or event that is being studied. The kernel design may be loosely compared to a stage setting. When the curtain opens for a play, the

1

audience becomes aware of the time, place, and setting of the play through action, stage scenery, and properties. Similarly, simple representations constructed out of cardboard can be used in the classroom at all grade levels to create an illusion of either (or both) time and place. For example, even a two-dimensional miniature of Big Ben rings out London; a picture or cardboard outline of the Eiffel Tower evokes an awareness of France; a crowded city skyline brings to mind the whole of any familiar big city; and the Statue of Liberty reminds one of New York. Given the basic steps for creating kernel designs, teachers can manipulate the classroom environment with free or inexpensive materials to make a specific unit of study come alive. It is not necessary that a teacher become a set designer or interior decorator; each teacher can learn an approach to design simplification and implementation that can result in a truly creative classroom environment.

The ultimate development of the kernel design is shown in the classroom, where most elements of manipulative decor, such as bulletin boards, blackboards, instructional centers, and seating arrangements reflect the time, place or concept being studied. When simplified, the scenographic pieces simply form highlights and specific clues from which to generalize the nature of the concept. Like the scenographic elements which support the actor in his efforts on the stage, the kernel design provides additional stimulus to the child in researching and role-playing many of his learning experiences.

The value of a creative classroom environment is gaining increasing support in educational literature. It is the heart of open education, the integrated day, and the interdisciplinary approach to learning. It provides many opportunities for a growing, responsible independence with each child gradually accepting more responsibility for his own learning and assuming greater self-direction. Creative classroom environments not only serve the child's emotional development but "also encourage intellectual development by giving opportunities for experimentation, exploration, and self-knowledge" (Mills & Mills 1972, p. 277). The creative classroom environment fulfills the criteria outlined by Torrance and Torrance (1973) for creative thinking: "the most successful approaches to creative thinking seem to be those that involve both cognitive and emotional functioning, provide adequate structure and motivation, and give opportunities for involvement, practice and interaction with teachers and other students" (p. 46).

According to Mayesky, et al. (1975), the child has an instinctive way of dealing with reality. He needs no written lines to memorize or structured behavior patterns to imitate in order to fantasize his world. "What he does need is an interesting environment and freedom to experiment and be himself" (p. 120). Fisher and Robertson (1940) likewise emphasize the importance of a rich, challenging environment in terms of "guarding, nurturing, releasing, and developing children's personalities" (p. 4).

The idea of a kernel design is related to the philosophies of Rousseau, who asserted that education is living; Dewey, who advocated that learning results from doing; Montessori, who emphasized the importance of the environment and the need for children to learn through the testimony of their senses; and Zirbes (1959), who maintained that "living, learning, and becoming are continuous and should be integratively related" (p. 76).

A creative environment does not necessarily teach a child what to think but rather assists him in how to think; a stimulating environment provides the motivation for a child to become a miniature researcher through the processes of reading, living, and recalling. This is extremely important when one considers the results of Mearns's study (1958) which showed that "those who are free from enough of the regimented type of learning to permit, under professional guidance, a sharing of the rugged labors of experimental and research-learning, learn more, retain longer, and learn more profitably" (p. 244).

The kernel design stimulates a child's discoveries and explorations. It helps him to develop a more complex frame of reference from which generalizations can be derived and applied to the present and future. Even though the teacher will probably be the initiator and master planner of the kernel design, children are still directed by their own curiosity and interest to search and discover relationships within the design. For example, in a unit on the Pilgrims, a teacher placed a large piece of cardboard representing the side of a building in one corner of the classroom. Windows were cut approximately four inches from the top. The third and fourth graders spent days researching books and viewing filmstrips to discover what the building represented and why the windows were placed so close to the top of the building. Some of the children even had their parents searching with them for the answers in the family encyclopedia. Through this type of active involvement with the stage set, or kernel design, children draw out the generalizations within the material. Through conversation with the teacher the child has the opportunity to express something about his experience. The teacher has the opportunity to ask critical questions to help the child become aware of patterns and relationships that he or she intuitively observed but could not clearly define.

THE KERNEL DESIGN AS A STAGE FOR ROLE-PLAYING

The creative classroom environment, based on the kernel design concept, provides a stage for role-playing. Role-playing is made easier and more meaningful when the classroom suggests in some way the appropriate atmosphere. "The setting of the stage by the teacher often acts as a motivation for the children to play" (Spodek 1972, p. 67). The developing child's early acting or role-playing provides a very vital source of social identification and understanding by which language acquisition and imagery and creative expressions are enriched (Hawley 1974; Spodek 1972). The child creates and expands his own changing representations and perceptions of reality when he combines written and verbal expressions with activity. "Acting within and upon their environment, children create a world for themselves and, in due time, re-create the world shared by all" (Frazier 1976, p. 279).

In Guidelines for the Preparation of Teachers of English (1968), Shugrue places importance on drama and/or role-playing in language acquisition. The guidelines state that drama can serve as the centrality of pupils' exploring, extending and shaping experiences in the classroom; drama meets the urgency of developing classroom approaches that stress the vital, creative dramatic movement of young people in language experiences, and it provides young people at all levels with significant opportunities for the creative uses of language - creative dynamics, imaginative writing, improvisation, role-playing, and similar activities.

Tyas (1971) feels there is an essential need in this computer age to educate the child to be aware of his creative powers and to be helped to realize these powers. "We can offer the child this important opportunity through child drama by re-creating with him, and for him, varied situations and different environments within the walls of the classroom. The child gains out of these experiences an improved ability to listen, to think creatively, to concentrate, to express his ideas freely and coherently, and to accept his responsibility to himself and to others" (p. V).

Barnes (1966) also relates the value of drama in preparing children to cope more effectively with a wide range of social opinions, attitudes, and evaluations. He describes our society as partaking of the "nature of drama: it speaks not with one voice but with many, and these often contradict one another in ways that not even the wisest of us can resolve" (p. 1). He feels that this society with its contradictory voices resides not only outside but within each one of us. Drama can serve as a means to help each person "learn to tolerate the many voices within himself, to recognize and express his own variousness, and to learn how to live amongst uncertainties and divided loyalties" (p. 1). Ward (1950) emphasizes the role of role-playing in terms of helping children to think independently and to grow through vicarious life experiences. The child's acting represents not only spontaneous reactions to the world that surrounds him and the expression of images that he has of this world, but it also reflects his own personal experiences, his inner self feelings, attitudes, and values.

Wolfson (1967) maintains that values can be learned by young children through role-playing, creative dramatics, literature, and art experiences. She feels that value development can be promoted by providing a wide variety of opportunities for individual selection of goals and activities and by allowing children to consider alternatives and possible consequences of acts as well as opportunities to consider their own feelings.

Child drama has been compared by Tyas (1971) to a voyage of self-discovery. The child is the captain; the adult is merely the navigator. Children are afforded opportunities to experiment with the use of their creative power and in the process are challenged to discover their individual self and potentiality. This self-discovery, as an outcome of role-playing, is also emphasized by Allstrom (1970). Fisher and Robertson (1940) maintain that children's acting provides opportunity for experiences contributing to all-around growth and fosters individual development of the kind which makes for successful social living.

Gray and Mager (1973) relate the importance of role-playing to individual development. They maintain that improvisation must not be left only to those teachers with acting talent and training; rather, every child should be provided with role-playing opportunities and techniques for becoming what he can be.

Role-playing serves as an important means to the development of the socialization skills (Rugg & Shumaker, 1928; Allstrom, 1970; Tyas, 1971; McCaslin, 1972; Hawley, 1974). "The process of socialization is inextricably woven into play activities" (Langford & Rand 1975, p. 185). "Though the children are pretending, they are learning to live together harmoniously, and this alone is an invaluable experience for them" (Hartman & Shumaker 1932, p. 265).

Role-playing helps children to see the viewpoints of other people. According to Mayesky et al. (1975) when feelings and emotions come out in role-playing, sensitive and open discussions following the role-playing offer new insights and learning. "This is a good way to help young children explore their feelings and find ways to handle their emotions and their relationships with others" (p. 121). McCaslin (1972) concurs that drama helps children learn about other people and sensitizes them to the feelings of others.

The basic needs of belongingness and security are often met as children plan and act out in an environment that heightens their imaginations. Tyas (1971) feels that because each child's response in role-playing is a valid individual expression, the child understands that he is only in competition with himself and thus gains a sense of security. He also becomes aware of how to motivate and discipline himself and his emotions, both in his own behavior and in his relations with others.

In view of the strong research approach for role-playing in the learning process, the idea of a creative classroom as a stage gains greater credibility. Role-playing becomes natural when the kernel design suggests the time, place, and setting. Role-centered activities, which are the core of an integrated unit, are fostered through the kernel design. It can help children identify themselves with the emotional experiences of the people about whom they are reading and studying. These emotional experiences will be remembered far longer than the mere researched facts.

THE TEACHER'S ROLE IN THE KERNEL DESIGN APPROACH

The teacher's role in the kernel design approach is similar to that of a teacher in any classroom in which children's involvement in the learning process is the primary goal. The teacher's responsibility is to establish an environment which encourages exploration, discovery, and investigation; an environment which challenges students to become critical problem solvers and decision makers; an environment that is planned around the integration of understandings, skills, attitudes, and appreciations related to significant real-life themes. Frazier (1976) concurs that active learning requires "a lush environment rich in alternatives rather than a restricted environment structured to assure the achievement of preselected ends" (p. 279). Within a truly creative classroom environment the teacher assumes the multivarious roles of a guide, a questioner, a listener, an interactor, a motivator, a planner, a researcher, and a resource person. Recent research supports each of these roles.

Smith and Torrance (1967) maintain that the role of the teacher is to set the conditions for creativity to happen. Because creativity is a quality deeply embedded in the human personality, it can be developed by reinforcement when it does happen, but the main function of the creative teacher is to maintain certain physical, psychological, socioemotional and intellectual conditions within the classroom so that creativity will be free to rise to the surface where it can be reached and developed. To effectively encourage creativity, the teacher needs to be interested in fostering curiosity, independence, and self-reliance (Goodale 1970).

Crosscup (1966) defines the role of the teacher in terms of relating to the child's active, inner life, with his attachments and scars, his evaluations and desires. The teacher needs to draw on this inner life, to help the child channel it and "find the forms by which a bridge can be built between his educational purposes for the child and the child's own inner life" (p. 240). This requires that the teacher provide activities which are potentially rich in meaning to the child.

Hertzberg and Stone's (1971) description of the role of the teacher as resource person in the open classroom is very applicable to the role of the teacher who uses the kernel design approach. "The teacher plays a decisive role in the experiences that are open to the child. It is the teacher who brings in the variety of materials from which a range of choices can be made, and it is up to the teacher to make the broadest possible range available for each child" (p. 9).

Rathbone (1971) likewise addresses the role of the teacher as resource person. He feels that the teacher's function is not to present answers; rather, it is to offer opportunities within which the child will generate his own satisfactory answers. "The teacher needs to prepare and present places where learning is likely to occur; he himself acts as a resource within these many overlapping learning environments offered to the child" (p. 107).

The teacher's role of resource person is critical to the success of the kernel design approach. Together the teacher and the students expand the appropriate illusion for the time and event being studied. This requires research in order to design and arrange properties that facilitate the action of the selected theme. This expanding process is part of the learning process. The teacher's role in this expanding process becomes that of a librarian and resource person. The teacher needs to make available a large collection of learning resources from which students can select to do small-group research projects. This array of materials helps to meet the various readiness and interest levels of the children; it allows the children to proceed at all levels of research activities and to proceed easily because the learning resources are immediately at hand for use at any moment in the day.

Information derived from a wide assortment of sources serves as a basis for establishing exciting new relationships within the kernel design. The role of the teacher is to guide the group-inquiry process, using perplexing subject matter and resource material as a means for developing clearer insights and relationships (Wendel, 1973). The relationships are integral to helping the child rethink, redefine, reconstruct, and renew basic understandings and ideas.

Crosscup (1966) views the role of the teacher as a guide in helping children make exciting discoveries. He feels it cannot be assumed that a child will make exciting discoveries if the adult simply lets matters rest and does not help him see that a discovery is needed. On the other hand, the adult cannot possibly make such a discovery for the child - the child must be guided to do this for himself. Similarly, Herbert Spencer advocated that children should be led to make their own investigations and to draw their own inferences. They should be told as little as possible and induced to discover as much as possible. The role of the teacher is not to promote optimal conditions for transmission of knowledge but "to extend the range of possibilities children can explore" (Barth 1972, p. 74).

Teacher guidance is paramount. For a student to direct his own learning successfully, "he needs close and systematic guidance from teachers who know him well - his interests, attitudes, values, and abilities" (Buckman 1973, pp. 54-55). Leitman (1968) draws an analogy between the teacher's role and that of a travel agent. He helps a child to go where the child wants to go. He counsels on the best way of getting there.

Barth (1972) refers to the role of the teacher as an "ad hoc responder" who "constantly scans the horizon of children's interactions with materials and with one another, for situations when a response, an appropriate intervention, will contribute to a child's learning" (p. 107). Similarly Bott et al. (1969) define the role of the teacher as a "mediator of experience who looks on every aspect of children's living as a means of learning" (p. 184).

Seaburg and Zinsmaster (1972) compare the role of the teacher to the role of a director in the performing arts. The teacher, like the director, envisions and develops an overall plan of action but finds that as he works with the participants he must make changes. The teacher, also, must observe the pupils as they become involved with the materials and so pick up clues for change. Thus the artist/teacher knows the materials and envisions them, but lets part of his plan emerge as he works with the particpants. "The teacher, like the director, must develop the ability to look at materials and see them 'come to life.' The teacher must also consider the significance of material in relationship to pupils, where they live, and the time in which they live" (p. 173).

Thoreau once said, "To affect the quality of the day, that is the highest of arts." Similarly, the ultimate role in the art of teaching is to affect the quality of the day for each child. Concern for quality is basic to the various roles the teachers play in the kernel design approach. Classroom management sugggestions that help facilitate these various roles are discussed in Chapter 2.

PROCEDURES FOR IMPLEMENTING THE KERNEL DESIGN APPROACH

The kernel design technique is offered as a way to help teachers to stage the creative classroom. There are four procedural steps involved in developing the kernel design.

Step 1: Synthesizing a narrative statement typifying the area being studied.

The narrative statement serves as a summary of the salient features, qualities or characteristics of the specific area being studied. It is similar to the review of the material that a teacher would make prior to developing any lesson plan. The narrative description is important, since the kernel design construction reflects the major ideas outlined in the descriptive summary. Sample narrative statements have been prepared for each of several units fully described in the later chapters. These units are illustrative of what can be done with any social studies and most science units. Actually, the school district's regular curriculum guide for social studies serves as the basis for the chronological selection of the topics. In fact, teachers could be encouraged to follow their own social studies textbook for the selection of topics in order to avoid the repetition of the same unit at a different grade level. In the major social studies curriculum series, the information included in the teacher's manual provides background information that can be used in synthesizing the narrative statement.

<u>Step 2:</u> Researching illustrations depicting the area being studied.

The second step in kernelization is to research illustrations depicting the area being studied. The simplest research tools can often be used to locate usable illustrations: encyclopedias, basic histories, brochures from travel agencies, picture files in the public library, children's books, or pictorial magazines. In the process of researching the illustrations, one needs to take a cursory, surface look at each illustration and ask what unique element is there which, out of context, will still remind us of the area or time being studied? For example, a pointed Gothic arch and a Rose window may evoke both a broad period in time (the thirteenth to sixteenth centuries) and the emotional context of a church.

<u>Step 3:</u> Kernelizing the uniqueness of the specific area being studied using the narrative statement and illustrations.

In kernelizing the ideas, the challenge is to capture a simplified portion of each illustration that speaks of the unique era being studied. When Thoreau went to Walden Pond he said he wanted to drive life into the barest corner and reduce it to its lowest terms to find out if it was really worth living. "Simplify, simplify, simplify," he said, "so that things will be reduced to their essence - and thus they can be examined for their true and elemental value." Similarly, the key word in developing a kernel design is "simplify." Reduce actuality to next to nothing, but keep it recognizable for what it is. This sounds impossible, but it can be done. If properly done, there is at least one hidden benefit - the construction and finishing of the kernel design elements will be all the simpler for good planning and careful design reduction.

<u>Step 4:</u> The drafting of the kernel design

The initial step in drafting the design is to visualize pieces or cutouts from the original illustrations, so that when seen isolated and out of context, they will always evoke the full illustrations of the original designs in one's memory. Although somewhat more difficult to do when trying to kernelize people in action, the same process may be used. One must focus on the details of costume, unique properties such as the sari, the turban, the scarf, the marketplace, or the community with people in action. Practical suggestions for visualizing and creating a kernel design are found in Chapter 12.

Creating an atmosphere conducive of a mood or a time or a place in the complete, naturalistic style often seen on the legitimate stage is actually easier in some ways than evoking the same level of response from a sketch or a fragment of scenery. If we assume the teacher has advanced scenographic skills, the re-creation of an actual place should present few problems, for photographs or drawings may be mechanically reproduced on paper as working drawings and then executed as a full-sized or scaled replica of the original. But how often do we find teachers with any scenographic skills or classrooms barely large enough to seat all the children with little room left to house theatrical scenery? It is possible, however, to develop an understanding of simplification and, by practice, arrive at a level of skill by which fragmentary but highly evocative pieces may be placed in the classroom in an economical fashion.

Great drafting skills are not required for creating the kernel design. The teacher need not be a master artist; in fact, the teacher need not even know how to draw. Three very simple ways of outlining the kernel design are available: the overhead projector can be used by making a transparency of one of the illustrations and masking out the portions that are not necessary to evoke the image unique to the era or place being studied; the opaque projector can be used to draw the outline on the cardboard; or slides of a place can be taken and projected on a cardboard for making the outline. Use of any of these techniques eliminates the precise scaling process employed in theatrical stagecraft. Other simplified techniques of stagecraft which extend the teacher's ability to plan the classroom more effectively and efficiently are included in Chapter 12.

Materials required for creating the illusions of time and space are very minimal, free, or inexpensive. Large refrigerator cartons, intact or unfolded, can be painted with tempera and manipulated with scissors or matte knives. Further, the skeletal ideas may be disassembled and reduced to smaller pieces and saved. Masking tape can be used to assemble or reassemble the various parts. Slides of the completed project will help the teacher to reassemble the kernel design at a future time. Depending on the size of the classroom, teachers can decide whether the kernel design will consume floor space or be suspended from the ceiling. It is possible to reduce virtually all kernel designs so that they can be suspended. If classroom space is not a problem, then, perhaps, the topic itself will suggest the appropriateness of using floor space.

Once the design has been drafted, children can become vitally involved in filling in the details and in proving through their research and numerous small-group activities that the design is indeed indigenous to the society, era, or topic being studied. While the teacher anticipates certain generalizations, children prove them. They utilize the threefold technique of research: identifying ideas, analyzing them, and generalizing. Thus the slogan "Read it, live it, recall it" becomes significant in this strong research and role-playing approach.

SUMMARY

The kernel design is basically scenographic. It is a method of unifying the classroom by means of simplified scenic or graphic set pieces depicting a time-place relationship or other concept. Originally designed as an aid to the study of social developments, the kernel design has been shown to be effective in supporting science projects as well.

The traditional passive classroom yields to an environment that reflects the excitement of today's active world. Likewise, the traditional role of the teacher as instructor and imparter of knowledge yields to the multivarious roles of the teacher as guide, questioner, listener, interactor, motivator, resource person, and designer of a creative, stimulating environment.

The ultimate development of the kernel design is shown in the classroom where most elements of manipulative decor, bulletin boards, blackboards, seating arrangements and instructional centers reflect the time, place or concept being studied. When simplified, scenographic pieces kernelized from joint teacher-pupil research, simply form highlights, specific clues from which to generalize the nature of the concept. Like the scenographic elements which support the actor in his efforts on the stage, the kernel design approach provides additional stimulus to the child in role-playing many of his learning experiences, so that "living, learning, and becoming are indeed continuous and integratively related" (Zirbes 1959).

REFERENCES

Allstrom, E. You can teach creatively. New York: Abingdon Press, 1970.

Barnes, D. Drama in the English classroom. Champaign, Ill.: The Dartmouth Seminar Papers, National Council of Teachers of English, 1966.

Barth, R.S. Open education and the American school. New York: Agathon Press, 1972.

Bott, R.; Davies, M.P.; Jones, M.L.; Hitchfield, E.M.; Johnson, J.E.L.; and Tamburini, J.R. Fundamentals in the first school. Oxford: Froebel Institute of Education, 1969.

Buckman, P. Education without schools. London: Souvenir Press, 1973.

Crosscup, R. Children and dramatics. New York: Charles Scribner's Sons, 1966.

Fisher, C., and Robertson, H.G. Children and the theater. California: Stanford University Press, 1940.

Frazier, A. Teaching children today: An informal approach. New York: Harper & Row, 1976.

Goodale, R.A. "Methods for encouraging creativity in the classroom," Journal of Creative Behavior, Vol. 4, No. 2 (1970), pp. 91-102.

Gray, F., and Mager, G. Liberating education. California: McCutchan, 1973.

Hartman, G., and Shumaker, A. Creative expression. New York: John Day, 1932.

Hawley, R.C. Value exploration through role-playing. Amherst, Mass.: Educational Research Associates, 1974.

Hertzberg, A., and Stone, E.F. An American approach to the open classroom: Schools are for children. New York: Schocken Books, 1971.

Langford, L., and Rand, H. Guidance of the young child. New York: Wiley, 1975.

Leitman, A. Travel agent: Housing for early childhood education. Bulletin No. 22-A. Washington, D.C.: Association for Childhood Education International, 1968.

Mayesky, M.E.; Neuman, D.B.; and Flodkowski, R. Creative activities for young children. New York: Delmar, 1975.

McCaslin, N. Creative dramatics in the classroom. New York: McKay, 1972.

Mearns, H. Creative power: The education of youth in the creative arts. New York: Dover, 1958.

Mills, H., and Mills, R. Designing instructional strategies for young children. Dubuque, Iowa: William C. Brown, 1972.

Rathbone, C., ed. Open education: The informal classroom. New York: Citation Press, 1971.

Rugg, H., and Shumaker, A. The child-centered school. Cleveland, Ohio: World Book, 1928.

Seaburg, D., and Zinsmaster, W. "What can teachers learn from directors in the performing arts?" Elementary School Journal, Vol. 72, No. 4 (1972), pp. 167-175.

Shugrue, M., and Everetts, E. "Guidelines for the preparation of teachers of English," English Journal (1968), pp. 475-564.

Smith, J., and Torrance, E.P. Creative teaching of the creative arts. New York: Allyn & Bacon, 1967.

Spodek, B. Teaching in the early years. Englewood Cliffs, N.J.: Prentice-Hall, 1972.

Torrance, E.P., and Torrance, J.P. Is creativity teachable? Indiana: Phi Delta Kappa Editions, 1973.

Tyas, B. Child drama in action. New York: Drama Book Specialists/Publishers, 1971.

Ward, W. Theatre for children. London: The Children's Theatre Press, 1950.

Wendel, R. "The teacher's dilemma with the open classroom," Education Digest, Vol. 94, No. 2 (Nov./Dec. 1973), pp. 53-56.

Wolfson, B.J. "Values and the primary school teacher," Social Education, Vol. 31, No. 1 (1967), pp. 37-38.

Zirbes, L. Spurs to creative teaching. New York: G.P. Putnam's Sons, 1959.

SUPPLEMENTARY BIBLIOGRAPHY

Berger, P., and Luckman, T. The social construction of reality. New York: Anchor, 1966.

"Bibliography on puppets for elementary school," The Speech Teacher, Vol. 3, No. 3 (1953).

Britton, J. Language and learning. Baltimore, Md.: Penguin, 1970.

Burger, I.B. Creative play acting. 2nd ed. New York: Ronald Press, 1966.

Burke, K. Language as symbolic action. Berkeley: University of California Press, 1966.

Carlton, L., and Moore, R.   "Effects of self-directive dramatization on reading achievement and self-concept of culturally disadvantaged children." Reading Teacher, Vol. 20, No. 2 (1966) pp. 125-130.

Church, J. Language and the discovery of reality. New York: Random House, 1961.

Courtney, R. Play, drama and thought. London: Casell, 1968.

Crosscup, R.   Children and dramatics. New York: Charles Scribner's Sons, 1966.

Cuffaro, H.K. "Dramatic play - the experience of block building." The Block Book, edited by E.S. Hirsch. Washington, D.C.: National Association for the Education of Young Children, 1974.

Durland, F.C.   Creative dramatics for children.   Yellow Springs, Ohio: Antioch Press, 1961.

Elkonin, D.B. "Symbolics and its functions in the play of children." in Child's Play, edited by W.E. Herron and B. Sutton-Smith. New York: Wiley, 1971.

Erwin, E.   "Implications for a project utilizing creative dramatics with preschool children with cleft palates." Paper read at the American English Teachers' Association (AETA) Convention, August 1967, in New York City. Unpublished.

Fitzgerald, B. Let's act the story. San Francisco: Featon, 1957.

Gardner, H.   The arts and human development.   New York: Wiley-Interscience, 1973.

Goodman, N. Languages of art. Indianapolis: Bobbs-Merrill, 1968.

Gross, D. "Play and thinking." In Play: Children's Business. Washington, D.C.: Association for Childhood Educational International, 1963.

Haas, R.B.   Psychodrama and sociodrama in American education. Beacon, N.Y.: Beacon House, 1949.

Herron, W.E., and Sutton-Smith, B., eds.   Child's play. New York: Wiley, 1971.

Hirsch, E.S. The block book. Washington, D.C.: National Association for the Education of Young Children, 1974.

Kerman, G.L. Plays and creative ways with children. New York: Harvey House, 1961.

Lease, R., and Siks, G. Creative dramatics for home, school and community. New York: Harper Bros., 1952.

Mattick, I. "The teacher's role in helping young children develop language competence," Young Children, Vol. 27 (1972), pp. 133-142.

McIntyre, B.M. Informal dramatics. Pittsburgh: Stanwix House, 1963.

Millar, S. The psychology of play. Baltimore, Md.: Penguin, 1968.

Piaget, J. Play, dreams and imitation in childhood. New York: Norton, 1962.

Shapiro, E.K., with B. Biber. "The education of young children: A developmental-interaction approach," Teacher's College-Record, Vol. 74 (1972), pp. 55-79.

Siks, G. Creative dramatics. New York: Harper & Bros., 1958.

Siks, G., and Dunnington, H., eds. Children's theater and creative dramatics. Seattle: University of Washington Press, 1961.

Singer, J. The child's world of make-believe. New Haven: Yale University Press, 1973.

Slade, P. Child drama. London: University of London Press, 1954.

Sutton-Smith, B. "The expressive profile." In Towards New Directions in Folklore, edited by B. Paredes. Austin: University of Texas Press, 1972.

Thetbar, R. "Human Relations through creative dramatics." Paper read at the American English Teachers (AETA) Convention, 1966, in Chicago. Unpublished.

Walker, P.P. Seven steps to creative children's dramatics. New York: Hill & Wang, 1957.

Ward, W. Creative dramatics. New York: Appleton-Century-Crofts, 1930.

Weber, E. Early childhood education: Perspectives on change. Worthington, Ohio: Charles A. Jones, 1970.

2 An Ounce of Prevention Is Worth a Pound of Cure: Management Considerations

While this proverb may soon become an antiquated cliché as the United States converts to the metric system of measurement, its meaning is relevant and applicable to establishing a classroom environment in which children are actively involved in the learning process. Teachers need to anticipate certain managerial problems when changing to and maintaining an informal classroom setting. If the problems and needs are anticipated and handled decisively, the teacher will then be freed to work with the children, expanding the concepts with which they are experimenting rather than spending time on problems that could have been prevented. This chapter presents a rationale for management and offers some general principles for establishing a classroom environment as a stage. A look at what theorists are saying about the management of the informal classroom will support our rationale for the management of the creative classroom environment.

ESTABLISHING FREEDOM WITH RESPONSIBILITY

"The three keys - enrichment, freedom, and responsibility - can help to open the doors to a happy and meaningful classroom experience for teachers and children" (Berger & Winters 1973, p. 99). Theorists have defined freedom in various ways. Borton (1970) describes it as the students' ability to choose from alternatives. Students must win freedom for themselves because teachers cannot give it to them. "The best the teacher can do is to teach them the processes which will increase their ability to step aside from their own way of experiencing - to wonder at it, to question it, and to modify it" (p. 163). Similarly, Hawkins (1974) concurs that "freedom is related to opportunities for significant choice in the optimization of learning. Discipline is related to the very nature of subject-matter; it is accepted and prized as it is seen to extend the power of the learner, to increase his range of significant choice. Freedom and discipline together imply an environment which is rich in opportunities for their exercise" (p. 98).

According to Hertzberg and Stone (1971), discipline is maintained not

15

through threats or fear or pressure arising from one's "authority," but from factors present in the informal environment itself. Barth (1970) points out that in many British primary classrooms only two rules exist - no destroying equipment, and, no destroying or interfering with the work, play, and activities of other children. "A child's freedom has to be carefully balanced. Too much freedom and the child feels thwarted. The teacher tries to choose the right time to give 'do's and don'ts'" (Sutton 1970, p. 12). The teacher needs to combine firmness of purpose with a flexibility that enables him to change direction readily if necessary (Pullan et al. 1971).

Featherstone (1971), during his extensive visits to the schools in England, observed that children "accept the real and legitimate authority of a teacher as an adult responsible for making a nurturing environment in which children and their talents can grow" (p. 85). Barth (1972), in commenting on Duberman's position of the authority of the teacher in the British primary schools, states that "it is both a legitimate and necessary role of the adult in the open classroom to be an authority for the children - a source of accumulated experience, knowledge, insight, maturity, leadership, arbitration, strength, judgment, and stability. It is vital to the successful functioning of the open classroom that the teacher be an authority, without becoming an authoritarian" (p. 98).

Many theorists concur that there is a positive relationship between classroom control and the active involvement of children in the learning process. "Control is understood to rise out of and rest on the absorption of children in their work. The challenge is to see to it that children are well occupied" (Frazier 1976, p. 274). Ridgway and Lawton (1965) feel that boredom and frustration do not occur when children are involved in their work and the work is individually chosen or matched to the child's need and ability. "This, together with verbal freedom, and creative work and play with its fantasy-release, reduces the incidence of rebelliousness or defiant conduct to negligible proportions" (p. 133). Brown and Precious (1968) feel that "as the children become more absorbed in their activities and learn to cope with freedom, the noise level decreases" (p. 126). Pullan et al. (1971) caution that "vague ideas about 'free activity' that allow the children too wide a choice of occupation with insufficient follow-up or depth, may lead only to noisy restlessness, a sure sign that they are not deeply enough involved and that they have lost interest" (p. 43).

"Teachers need to learn to read the signs and symptoms of apparent restlessness and to deal promptly with underlying causes" (Frazier, p. 23). Lindberg and Swedlow (1976) suggest that teachers examine the materials children are using as a possible cause of disruptive behavior. The materials may be either too difficult or not challenging enough. Sometimes an appropriate question or suggestion will open up new challenges for the child to use the materials constructively.

Silberman (1970) feels that "in the informal classroom, the discipline problem withers away in part because children are not required to sit still and be silent" (p. 269). Ridgway and Lawton (1965) also discuss the value of involving children actively in learning as a basis for reducing discipline problems. They quote the headteacher of a large school where active involvement in the learning process is a major goal as saying, "The difficult ones become undifficult" (p. 133).

ESTABLISHING ROUTINES DURING THE INITIAL WEEKS

"A certain amount of management of children by adults, a certain amount of imposed order, structure and control is a necessary pre-condition for independent exploration. Reasonable consistent restrictions on children's behavior ultimately enables them to be more free and productive" (Barth 1972, p. 97). The importance of establishing classroom expectations from the start cannot be overemphasized. The first two to three weeks afford an opportunity to establish routines that will ensure that the creative environment approach to learning will run smoothly throughout the rest of the year.

Some of the basic routines that might be established during the initial weeks are the processes of selecting an activity, completing the selected activity, checking with the teacher when the activity is completed, and putting away the materials. Routines can be established for two situations that inevitably occur - some things are going to spill and other things are going to be broken or consumed. Children need to understand from the beginning that it helps the teacher to know when something needs repair or replacement. A box for this purpose could be placed in the classroom. Children write a note about needed materials. In this way teachers will not be interrupted during instructional time and children will develop a sense of responsibility for the supply and use of the materials. Hassett and Weisberg (1972) emphasize the need for the open classroom to be a well-organized, well-disciplined unit. They feel the "housekeeping must be meticulous, and the children must participate in organizing the disciplining, and the housekeeping, or there is danger of disintegration into chaos" (p. 52).

The initial two- to three-week period provides the teacher with an opportunity to assess the needs and interests of children. Brown and Precious (1968) emphasize the urgency of getting to know the children and their individual personalities and needs, since much of the stimulation of thought that comes from the classroom environment can only be effective if the books and materials reflect the wide range of interests represented in the respective classrooms.

During this initial readiness period, through praise and recognition of the child's completion of a task, the teacher helps to imbue each child with the confidence that he can be successful. What the teacher really wants is to make the completion of the task as rewarding as possible. The checking period should be a time of warm, friendly conversation between teacher and pupil. In time, this conversation will be the most rewarding part of the day because it is the most truly individualized time in the program, oriented entirely to the needs of the individual child. "These opportunities for 'teacher-child' interactions serve many purposes. They are used to further instruction and to provide information about the child as well as to communicate emotional support and assurance" (Spodek 1972, p. 1). Thomas (1975) feels the most important, most imperative single ingredient necessary to open up the classroom so that children express their freedom to learn is the relationship between teacher and pupils, and pupils and pupils. Similarly, Sabaroff and Hanna (1970) observe that "knocking walls out of buildings does not create open learning environments. Developing trust and good communication between adults and children and providing an appropriately stimulating and active environment does" (p. 104). Brown and Precious (1968) feel that mutual respect between teacher and child and the positive way in which children identify with their teacher explain to a great degree the lack of behavior problems in the informal classroom.

The child's attitude about his own ability begins to form during the initial three- to four-week period. He learns, regardless of his previous experiences, that his teacher believes in his ability and is very interested in his way of thinking and questioning. Within a supportive, positive atmosphere, the child grows to think of himself as a hard worker, one who persists at his work, even if it's difficult. He feels pride in the fact that he finishes his work and enjoys the freedom and responsibility he has during the worktime. He experiences freedom to move about, to select his own small group of independent work, to choose where he is going to do his work. He becomes aware of his responsibility for working during the time scheduled for it, for telling the teacher when he is finished and for putting away the materials so that they are ready for the next person who may choose to use them. Spodek's (1972) description of the teacher's role is applicable throughout the year but it is especially critical during these initial weeks when a creative classroom environment is being established. "The teacher's role as a professional would be to set the stage for learning, to provide legitimate alterntives for children's activities in school, and to serve as a guidance function in the classroom. The teacher would provide alternative goals, help them anticipate the consequences of their acts, help them evaluate their activities, and help to see that the school provides productive learning situations for all children" (p. 52).

Role-playing can be used during this initial preparation period to establish not only the "how" of the routines and rules but also the "why." For example, children could role-play how they can be of assistance to one another, what would happen if the children were allowed to shout across the room for the teacher's help whenever they wanted it, or, what happens when materials are not returned to their proper places or replaced when consumed. Role-playing can be used to teach respect for the materials and how "to use them properly, profitably, and economically" (Hassett & Weisberg, 1972, p. 32). Once the routines and expectations have been set, the teacher will be able to enjoy the benefits of an individualized program throughout the year. "Slow, small steps thoughtfully taken lead to small successes and to growing confidence. Upon these small successes, additional small successes can more easily be built. Behind almost every successful informal classroom lies a sequence of these small discrete successes" (Barth, 1972, p. 215). The small steps leading to routines and expectations should not be viewed as restricting the child. Rather, they free the child to live successfully in a classroom environment that respects his right to learn.

PLANNING: THE KEY TO SUCCESSFULLY STRUCTURING THE CLASSROOM AS A STAGE

Theorists concur that planning is the critical factor to informal education. An environment that is organized to promote optimal participation by all the children in the learning experience requires in-depth planning. According to Hassett and Weisberg (1972), "an environment conducive to learning is one in which all materials are readily accessible, guidelines and limitations are clearly spelled out, and duties and responsibilities are delineated. This kind of setup takes planning, discussion, and constant evaluation with the children" (p. 109). Thomas (1975) likewise emphasizes the need for cooperative planning with children.

> A smooth, cooperative functioning of activities and interrelationships in your classroom is not apt to occur without joint planning by you and your pupils since each pupil is involved in his own needs, interests, and intentions and not necessarily those of the classroom as a whole. As is true in any family, it is essential that all children are encouraged to discuss and expand on the means for effective realization of these attributes. Create then a classroom atmosphere in which each pupil has a constructive role. (Pp. 179-180) Genuine participation by pupils in the organization and learning experiences of the classroom is essential to its stability and a necessary ingredient for open learning. (p. 226).

Similarly, Berger and Winters (1973) refer to the cooperative role of teachers and students as co-learners, co-investigators, and co-workers in planning various aspects of the problem.

By its very nature, the kernel design approach involves children as co-planners, co-investigators, and co-workers. While the teacher initiates the original scenic concept, the children cooperatively plan with the teacher the research tasks and role-playing activities that are related to the actual creative scenographic environment.

Thomas (p. 181) emphasizes that daily teacher-pupil planning sessions are required if the teacher is to be successful in opening up the classroom. He feels effective planning can help to achieve the following goals:

- Clarify directions, procedures, management, and limitations of learning experiences;
- Increase pupils' knowledge and understanding of each other's contributions;
- Open interrelationships between teacher and pupils and pupils and pupils;
- Invite sharing of pupil responsibility for the purposes, procedures, and activities of the classroom;
- Develop pupils' capacities to make decisions;
- Stimulate teacher and pupils to help each other;
- Increase feelings of self-acceptance and adequacy on the part of both teacher and pupils;
- Develop mutual trust, respect, and cooperation between teacher and pupils;
- Build classroom unity, cohesiveness, and togetherness.

Although children do plan more of their own work in an informal classroom, the teacher, as the Plowden Report (1967) makes clear, must constantly ensure a balance within the day or week for both the class and the individuals. He must see that time is profitably spent and give guidance in its use. Similarly, with the kernel design approach the teacher's role as guide becomes very critical. Biggs and MacLean (1969) likewise emphasize the major role the teacher plays in planning variations in approach, in the interaction of children, and in the experiences provided for individual children, which is the essence of active learning. "This variety in the environment is sometimes provided by the children themselves, but more often by the teacher" (p. 55).

Berger and Winters (1973) describe what they call the complex job of planning in terms of a very personalized role for each teacher. The teacher's own experiences, life situations, trips and cultural activities, magazines and newspaper articles, radio and television programs, can be integrated into the lesson plans and shared, investigated, observed, listened to, read about, and discussed with the students. As such, Berger and Winters view the teacher as "a recycler of all kinds of things that now become a useful part of class activity" (p. 8).

Planning requires consideration of children's time. According to Frazier (1976), "time for wondering and questioning is a part of the process by which interests become purposes" (p. 281). Ridgway and Lawton (1965) emphatically state that "what our children need most of all is time. . . time to be happy - to feel secure; time to talk - to us and to each other; time to play; time to create and time to destroy; time to listen, to discover, to experiment and time just to stand and stare" (p. 102).

ESTABLISHING A FRAMEWORK FOR INTERDISCIPLINARY PLANNING

Interdisciplinary learning is at the heart of the kernel design approach. The treatises of Bruner (1960), Hanna, Potter, and Hageman (1963), Presno and Presno (1967), Hawkins (1974), strongly support interdisciplinary structure as the basis for significant educational curriculum. "Rigid division of the curriculum into subjects tends to interrupt the thought patterns of children, causes them to lose interest and prevents them from identifying the common elements in problem solving. These are among the many reasons why most learning experiences should cut across the traditional subject disciplines" (p. 197). In a good school there is a constant interflow of ideas between all subjects and activities, so that false distinctions between play and work, the arts and sciences, intelligence and imagination are broken down" (Allen 1970, p. 232). According to Rogers (1970), interdisciplinary learning "helps support and build the image of the school as a place where lifelike questions may be investigated as opposed to questions that may appear to be narrowly academic" (p. 289).

Skeel (1970) strongly advocates the interdisciplinary conceptual approach to learning but maintains that "teachers often have difficulty arranging an effective sequence of activities for programs based on concepts" (p. 80). Biggs and MacLean (1969) likewise address the great need yet the great difficulty teachers have in trying to help children see order and pattern in experience.

The "lesson plan tree" is offered as one way to facilitate interdisciplinary planning. The lesson plan tree (Cobes & Heck, 1977) is a bulletin-board map for planning and implementing interdisciplinary studies. Like any map, it shows both the destination and the numerous routes leading to and from this end point. It shows how each topic is graphically related to other topics and to the whole.

The lesson plan tree, cut out of construction paper, can be a mere outline of a tree or a realistic representation of a tree pinned to a bulletin board. Roots, trunk, and major branches identify major subject areas of investigation. The class then progressively adds smaller branches and pins on labels and leaves to designate the subdivisions. Most subdivisions will represent small-group research or experimental activities. Children can either select the activities or cooperatively plan with the teacher which activities they will pursue. Names of children can be placed on leaves and pinned next to the activities they have selected.

The tree serves as a motivational device, allowing each class member to understand how his or her contribution relates to the whole. "Understanding is heightened by helping children relate newly experienced art works to those already encountered" (Frazier, 1976, p. 154). So often, teaching becomes fragmented into parts because of discrete subjects and prescribed time tables whereas "learning is an undivided whole" (Biggs & MacLean 1969, p. 197).

Figure 2-1 serves as an example of the interdisciplinary structure.

The lesson plan tree illustrates a plan for studying the pioneer/Indian community. The historical influence on the Indians and the pioneers, their use of the environment for food, clothing, and shelter, and their ways of satisfying their social, recreational, and religious needs are charted graphically on the tree. Viewing the tree, one can readily see how the larger problem of contrasting and comparing communal life of the Indians with that of the pioneers grows out of a complexity of smaller problems. "When the problem approach is used as the basis for unit organization, the overall problem is analyzed into sub-problems and questions, the answers to which are necessary before the overall problem can be solved" (Hanna, Potter, & Hageman, 1963, pp. 233-234).

GENERATING AND RELATING SMALL-GROUP RESEARCH ACTIVITIES

"If educators are really searching for an educationally viable plan for teaching children, then they must commit themselves to procedures that encourage children to investigate the world around them in interesting and pleasurable ways" (Berger & Winters, 1973, p. 99). The primary purpose of the kernel design is to generate possibilities for numerous small-group research activities for students. Students research such exploratory questions as what the stage-craft pieces represent, why they were made a certain way, how they were made, what purposes they served, why the events took place, how conditions and events affected the people. Berger and Winters feel that exploratory questions help children "to understand and accept differences,

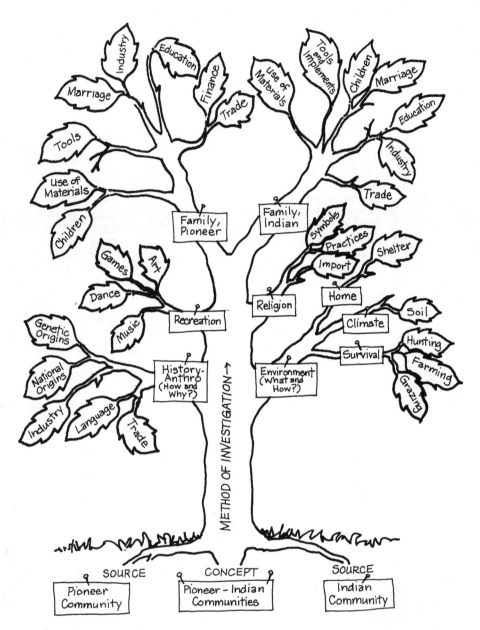

Fig. 2-1   The Lesson Plan Tree for Studying the Pioneer-Indian Community
(James Thorpe)

without judging whether a different way of life is better or worse than theirs" (p. 64).

According to Brearley (1969), "everything in a child's environment can be an object of intense curiosity to him and everything contains within it something from which he can learn" (p. 5). The teacher's role is to deepen that interest into knowledge. Brearley cautions, however, that this knowledge cannot be developed in a barren classroom. Rather, "children must bring their outside life into the classroom to get help in organizing it into a conceptual framework" (p. 5). Spodek (1972) concurs that "the world outside the classroom is also seen as a resource for children's learning. School experience goes beyond the four walls, bringing the world into the classroom and taking the class out into the real world" (p. 34). Similarly, Frazier (1976) maintains that "a workshop setting helps children continue to operate as natural learners. The world of wonders does not have to be left behind when school begins. Properly organized centers or areas excite and satisfy interest" (p. 14).

Small-group research activities, projects, experiments, problem-solving activities and role-playing activities can help bring the world into the classroom. Skeel (1970) addresses the value of small-group activities in relation to conceptual development: "the development of an understanding of the relationship of one subject area to another is made possible through integrating activities which help children realize that knowledge in one subject is related to other subject areas" (p. 66). An "interdisciplinary planning wheel" is offered as one suggestion for integrating activities. A large wheel can be pinned on a bulletin board or actually painted on the blackboard. The various social and physical sciences are placed along the circumference of the circle. (See Fig. 2-2.)

Related activities are placed within the appropriate wedges. A plastic acetate sheet can be placed over the wheel and students can write their names in the respective places to identify the activities they are researching. The interdisciplinary planning wheel is perhaps more valuable for the teacher than for students. The real value and utility of interdisciplinary structures according to Rogers (1970), "lies not in the creation of pre-packaged 'teacher proof curricula'; rather, it is the classroom teacher who must grasp them and utilize them at the appropriate moment. In other words 'structure' belongs in the minds of teachers" (p. 300). Furthermore, Rogers feels "if teachers grasp some of the insights of physical and social science, they will be able to help children see the generalized significance of events or phenomena that interest them. Similarly, they will be able to help children to ask questions that go beyond the merely descriptive; they will be able to see possibilities that may well have escaped them in the past" (p. 300).

Basic to designing small-group activities or interest-center tasks, is a consideration of the types of questions that will stimulate problem-solving processes. "Questions should be meaningful, emphasizing how and why, instead of what and when" (Berger & Winters, 1973, p. 64). Exploratory questions, such as, Why did the events take place? Why do people live and act as they do? and How do conditions and events affect people? can be typed on activity task cards for the children to research.

In addition to divergent, exploratory questions, activities and experiments which lead to discovery and exploration can be planned. Brainstorming with

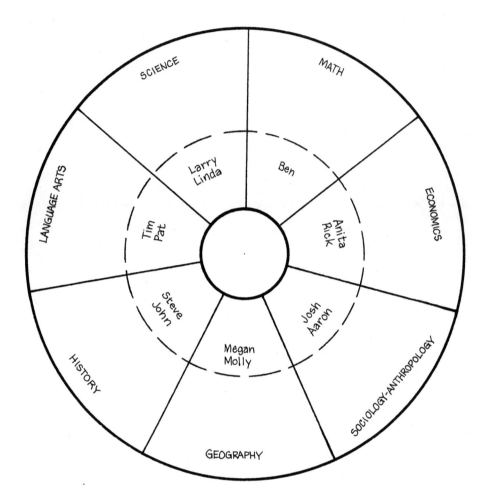

Fig. 2-2   Interdisciplinary Planning Wheel   (James Thorpe)

other teachers and students is perhaps one of the best ways to generate
numerous meaningful activities. In working with teachers, one of the authors
of this book found it useful to reprint the experiences which lead to student
learning as suggested by Brown et al. (1973).   Teachers brainstormed
activities to correspond with each of the learning behaviors. Often, just a list
of action verbs will help teachers to recall potential exploratory activities.
The list of learning experiences generated by Brown et al. (1973) includes the
following:

thinking	painting	viewing
discussion; speaking	drawing	exchanging
reporting	photographing	recording
reading	working	taping
writing	demonstrating	dramatizing
listening	experimenting	singing
interviewing	problem solving	imagining
outlining	collecting	judging
constructing	observing	evaluating
creating	playing	

"Knowledge of developmental processes can help us order the activities we provide for children in terms of what can be of use to a child at a particular level of development, and suggest what activities might proceed or follow others" (Spodek, 1972, p. 51). Pumerantz, Howell, and Galano (1974) also feel that in order to create meaningful activities in an informal classroom, "the teacher must have at her command an excellent understanding of child growth and development. In addition, she must firmly believe that the child has integrity and can be responsible to a great degree for his own learning" (p. 22).

Exploratory activities should include both individual activities and small-group activities. "Culminating activities draw together the learning experiences of the unit" (Skeel, 1970, p. 66). According to Frazier (1976), "attention to group activities is necessary in any program of informal teaching that strives for balance between depth and breadth" (p. 217). While the class may be divided into small groups to work on various activities within the creative atmosphere of a unified classroom, a culminating activity such as role-playing would bring the whole class together.

SUMMARY

"The three keys - enrichment, freedom, and responsibility," referred to by Berger and Winters (1973) as the way "to open doors to a happy and meaningful classroom experience for teachers and children" (p. 99), are integral to the creative classroom environment and the scenographic approach to unifying the classroom. Enrichment is achieved through the numerous small-group research activities that are designed to help children become critical problem-solvers; freedom is achieved by offering numerous alternatives from which the student can choose. Enrichment and freedom foster responsibility since "there must be opportunities for choice in what can be learned, because none of us can exercise responsibility without choice" (Muir 1970, p. 18).

When enrichment, freedom, and responsibility exist, the classroom becomes a place where children discover the joy of knowledge, the potential of ideas, and the fun of growing. Though the emphasis is on the free and happy experience of discovery and active involvement in the learning process, the classroom as a stage is structured and disciplined to make the most of the few short years when young minds are most receptive to ideas and, therefore, to learning.

REFERENCES

Allen, J. "Movement, music, drama and art," in Teaching in the British primary school, edited by V.R. Rogers. London: Collier-Macmillan, 1970.

Barth, R.S. Open education and the American school. New York: Agathon Press, 1972.

Berger, E., and Winters, B.A. Social studies in the open classroom: A practical guide. New York: Teacher's College Press, 1973.

Biggs, E.E., and MacLean, J.R. An active learning approach to mathematics. Reading, Mass.: Addison-Wesley, 1969.

Borton, T. Reach, touch and teach: Student concerns and process education. New York: McGraw-Hill, 1970.

Brearley, M., et al. Fundamentals in the first school. Oxford: Basil Blackwell, 1969.

Brown, J.R.; Lewis, R.; and Harcleroad, J.A.V. Instruction: Technology, media and methods. New York: McGraw-Hill, 1973.

Brown, M., and Precious, N. The integrated day in the primary school. London: Agathon Press, 1968.

Bruner, J.S. The process of education. Cambridge, Mass.: Harvard University Press, 1960.

Cobes, J., and Heck, S.F. "Lesson plan tree," The Science Teacher, Vol. 44, No. 1, (January, 1977), p. 40.

Featherstone, J. Schools where children learn. New York: Liveright, 1971.

Frazier, A. Teaching children today: An informal approach. New York: Harper & Row, 1976.

Hanna, L.A.; Potter, G.; and Hageman, N. Unit teaching in the elementary school. New York: Holt, Reinhart & Winston, 1963.

Hassett, J.D., and Weisberg, A. Open education: Alternatives within our tradition. Englewood Cliffs, N.J.: Prentice-Hall, 1972.

Hawkins, D. The informed vision: Essays on learning and human nature. New York: Agathon Press, 1974.

Hertzberg, A., and Stone, E.F. An American approach to the open classroom: Schools are for children. New York: Schocken Books, 1971.

Lindberg, L., and Swedlow, R. Early childhood education: A guide for observation and participation. Boston: Allyn & Bacon, 1976.

Muir, M. "How children take responsibility for their learning," in Teaching in the British primary school, edited by V.R. Rogers. London: Collier-Macmillan, 1970.

Plowden, Lady Bridget, et al. Children and the primary schools: A report of the Central Advisory Council for Education. London: Her Majesty's Stationery Office, 1967.

Presno, V., and Presno, C. Man in action series: People and their actions. Englewood Cliffs, N.J.: Prentice-Hall, 1967.

Pullan, J.M.; Norfield, E.J.; and White, W.L. Towards informality. New York: Citation Press, 1971.

Pumerantz, P.; Howell, B.; and Galano, R.W. Administrator's guide to the opening learning environment. West Nyack, N.Y.: Parker, 1974.

Ridgway, L., and Lawton, I. Family grouping in the primary school. New York: Agathon Press, 1965.

Rogers, V.R., ed. Teaching in the British primary school. London: Collier-

Macmillan, 1970.

Sabaroff, R., and Hanna, M.A. The open classroom: A practical guide for the teacher of the elementary grades. Metuchen, N.J.: The Scarecrow Press, 1970.

Silberman, C.D. Crisis in the classroom. New York: Random House, 1970.

Skeel, D.J. The challenge of teaching social studies in the elementary school. Pacific Palisades, Cal.: Goodyear, 1970.

Spodek, B. Teaching in the early years. Englewood Cliffs, N.J.: Prentice-Hall, 1972.

Sutton, A. Ordered freedom. Encino, Cal.: International Center for Educational Development, 1970.

Thomas, J.I. Learning centers: Opening up the classroom. Boston: Holbrook Press, 1975.

3 A Kernel Design of Prehistoric Indian Culture: Hopewell Indians

Most children and many adults have but a limited understanding of prehistoric or even colonial times. They need to be led through a process which temporarily erases from their inner vision concepts that accompany modern-day civilization. The kernel design technique can be used to help children better perceive the prehistoric world of man. For illustrative purposes, Ohio's prehistoric Hopewell Indian culture has been selected. However, this basic framework can be used in the study of any prehistoric culture.

In the period from approximately 10,000 B.C. to A.D. 1600, Ohio was inhabited more or less continuously by various groups of Indians. Each group had its own way of life, its own type of economy, art, social structure, and religion. Some groups were highly complex while others were simple, but all were reasonably successful at adapting themselves to their surroundings in the primitive setting of Ohio. A study of all the prehistoric cultures in this area would be impractical in a grade-school classroom; however, an in-depth study of one such group would give much overall information about prehistoric Indians in general and would help children to appreciate their rich and lengthy heritage.

NARRATIVE STATEMENT

The Hopewell Indians, or Mound Builders, who inhabited Ohio from roughly 300 B.C. to A.D. 600 represent the zenith of prehistoric Indian culture in Ohio. A powerful, highly organized culture (sometimes compared to but in no way associated with the Aztec culture of Central America), the Hopewells afford us the finest opportunity to study the customs and habits of prehistoric

---

* An earlier version of this chapter was published as "All the Classroom is a Stage: An Experiential Approach to the Study of Ohio's Prehistoric Indian Culture" in The Ohio Council for the Social Studies Review (Spring 1977), No. 13.

Indians of the Ohio country.

Prehistoric Ohio was a forest wilderness, mutilated first by the advancement and then by the retreat of the Wisconsin glacial stage. All evidence of civilization and mechanization was absent. In this postglacial setting lived stone age man, clannish and nomadic, following moving herds in his endless search for food, carrying only utilitarian stone tools. No written language was developed by any prehistoric or later Indian culture, binding the Indians securely to the Stone Age.

Into this setting, following several thousand years of primitive Indian inhabitation, came the peaceful, powerful, highly organized Hopewell Indians. Their culture was a sedentary one, occupying permanent villages and relying upon farming in addition to hunting for subsistence. The Hopewells had a highly developed social organization divided into clans and other formal groups and were dominated by a ruling class.

The most elaborate burial customs of any of the prehistoric groups in the region, or perhaps in North America, were practiced by the Hopewells. Much ceremony was involved in the "cult of the dead" ritual related to the Hopewell religion. This ritual was presided over by the shaman, or priest, thought to be the most powerful figure in Hopewell society.

The large, often curvilinear earthworks of the Hopewell left an indelible mark on the landscape of Ohio. They are among the most spectacular Indian sites in North America. The burial mounds erected over their dead number more than ten thousand in Ohio. Effigy earthworks, great earthen walls, and geometric enclosures are outstanding examples of the Hopewells' ability to plan large-scale construction projects and to organize the manpower to build them using only primitive stone age tools.

The Hopewells were unique in early cultures for the beautiful ornaments and implements they made from stone, copper, mica, shell, and bone. In order to acquire these materials, they carried on considerable commerce with other parts of the country, establishing themselves as capable traders by obtaining mica from the Carolinas, obsidian and grizzly teeth from the Rocky Mountains, ocean shells and shark teeth from the Gulf of Mexico, and copper from Michigan. Their skillful artisans wove fabric from wild grasses and vegetable fibers, created pottery for storage of food and supplies, and supplied flint and bone tools for all utilitarian purposes.

RESEARCHING ILLUSTRATIONS

Illustrations of Hopewell Indian life are found mostly in conjunction with actual sites of Hopewell earthworks, in museums built upon these sites and in books published by the Ohio Historical Society. Perhaps the finest source of information is the re-creation of prehistoric Indian life on exhibit at the Ohio Historical Center in Columbus. Books, brochures, and picture postcards depicting these re-creations are available, as are filmstrips and slides. Material concerning the use of flint by prehistoric Indians is available from Flint Ridge State Memorial, near Zanesville, Ohio. These materials would be useful not only for the teacher in selecting kernel designs, but also for the children to use in researching information.

KERNELIZING IDEAS AND DESIGNING RELATED RESEARCH
ACTIVITIES, PROJECTS AND EXPERIMENTS

In kernelizing the ideas, the challenge is to capture a simplified portion of each illustration that speaks of the Hopewell Indians. The first kernel design for a unit on the Hopewell Indian, a forest setting, is intended to help create for the children a concept of the primitive Indian's relationship to and dependence upon his environment. A simplified forest setting, depicted in Fig. 3-1, can be cut from a large piece, or several pieces of cardboard and painted with forest greens and browns.

Fig. 3-1   The Kernel Design of the Forest   (James Thorpe)

Depending on the size of the classroom, the forest can either be suspended from the ceiling or placed on the floor. A large yellow sun can be suspended from the ceiling to help represent dependence on sunshine and rain. Laid upon the floor, blue crepe paper or cloth can represent a river or lake near which the Indian always camped or lived, because both he and the game he hunted needed a water supply for survival. With this setting children can re-create through role-playing the prehistoric Indian's struggle for survival as he used only the materials found in nature, totally dependent upon his ingenuity and cunning.

Numerous small-group activities relate to this simple introductory kernel design of the forest. They lay the foundation for successful understanding of remaining kernel designs. They include the following:

1.   Have children research how the Indian came to North America. They could trace the route followed on a map of the world which could then be displayed for future reference in the study. Research should answer such questions as: How was the Indian able to cross from Asia to Alaska? Why did he come? Why was he unable to return to Asia? Why did the isolated Indian groups in North and South America develop different cultural habits?

2.   To aid in the perception of the great span of prehistoric time, have children construct a time line in the form of a Hopewell spear. A real or facsimile spearhead is bound to a wooden shaft with rope or leather binding so the overall length is 36 inches. Important dates are marked by heavy lines on the spear.

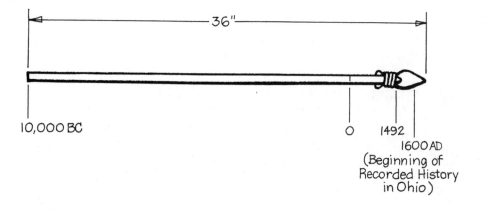

Fig. 3-2   Spearhead   (James Thorpe)

3.   Have children research and report on the meaning of Stone Age and the level of civilization it represents.

4.   Have children research and report on the present-day Stone Age culture, bringing illustrations so children can see the simplicity and primitive nature of this lifestyle. If possible, display illustrations in the classroom throughout the study, symbolizing the fact   that for

some, the Stone Age still exists today.

5.   Display a time scale which compares the prehistoric Indian cultures of Ohio to events and discoveries happening simultaneously elsewhere in the world.

6.   Since the first prehistoric Indians came into Ohio following the retreat of the Wisconsin glacial age, a child could research this last ice age. On a world globe he could cover with cotton that part of the world covered by the Wisconsin glacier. The globe should remain on display for reference throughout the study. Evidence of glacial action in Ohio, such as the grooved rocks on Kelly's Island, could be discussed with illustrations of the grooves displayed. Conduct a discussion on the ramifications of the possibility of the approach of another ice age.

7.   Have children research and report on the animals, now extinct, which were hunted by early prehistoric man, for example, mammoth, mastodon, giant beaver, giant elk, giant sloth, musk ox, tapir. Illustrations should be displayed for all animals discussed.

8.   Illustrate the size of prehistoric game animals by displaying a full-scale cutout of the femur of the mastodon next to a life-sized cutout of a man with the femur exposed. A number of illustrations of this kind can be instructive, for they will appeal to the child as a less complex concept than that of the passage of time, while at the same time gently leading to more difficult concepts by building and maintaining interest in the general subject.

The kernel design of the forest setting now becomes the background setting for the kernel design of the Hopewell dwelling place, distinctively styled, symbolic of the sedentary existence of the highly developed Hopewell culture. Cut from a large piece of cardboard to resemble the design in Fig. 3-3, the dwelling place can be braced to stand on the floor in front of the forest setting or suspended from the ceiling if space is at a premium.

Large sticks can be fastened to the cardboard to resemble the pole supports, ridgepole, and braces of the dwelling place. The arched roof can be thatched with grasses, bark, and mud. The blue cloth or crepe paper continues to represent a nearby water supply. Dirt on the floor in front of the dwelling, sticks arranged to resemble a fireplace, pottery vessels, and burlap sacks representing the animal hides used for bedding and comfort help to complete the kernel design of Hopewell housing. No form of furniture is used. All activity takes place on the floor. Within this kernel design, children can act out the family routine of the Hopewell life, identifying the difficulties inherent in this primitive lifestyle.

Suggestions for activities include:

1.   Hopewell dwellings were fashioned in a particular, distinctive style. Children could research this style and build a miniature model to show the pole structure, using bark, sticks, and grasses as an authentic covering for the roof and sides. This model could be kept on display for reference throughout the study and could serve as a guide

for the erection of the kernel design of the dwelling place.

2. Children could research the many uses Indians made of the animals they killed, emphasizing that no usable part of the animal was wasted. A list could be made of these uses and displayed in the room.

3. The Hopewell Indians used pottery for storage of food and supplies and as vessels for carrying water. Children could research and demonstrate the Hopewell method of making pottery by coiling rolls of grit-tempered clay to form the desired object, which is then pounded to shape. Pottery objects could be decorated to resemble authentic Hopewell pottery, fired and displayed.

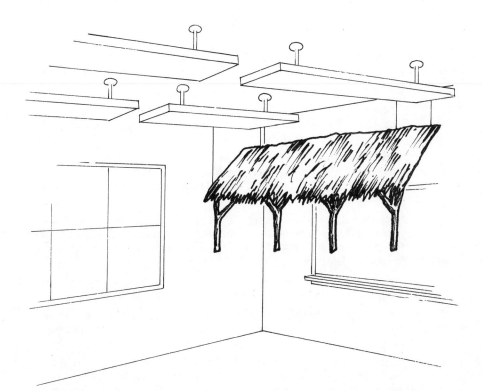

Fig. 3-3   The Kernel Design of the Hopewell Dwelling Place   (James Thorpe)

4. Children could research the food-gathering habits of the Hopewells. Corn, roots, seeds, and berries could be displayed. Corn or sunflower seeds could be ground with a pestle or hammerstone against flat or hollow rock.

5.   The Hopewell Indians wove fabric of bark, wild grasses, and wild vegetable fibers. Children could gather these materials and practice weaving them. The finished "cloth" could be displayed.

6.   Children could research theories about the type of clothing, jewelry and hairstyles worn by the Hopewell people. Children could make authentic-looking costumes of brown paper or burlap, could fashion jewelry facsimiles such as ear spools, gorget necklaces, and copper bracelets.

7.   Children could plant a patch of corn in a section of the schoolyard, using only primitive stone celts and shell hoes to prepare the ground. The corn plants should be cultivated with these tools also, accenting the awkwardness and inefficiency of primitive farming methods.

Flint is perhaps the one most valuable natural material used universally by all prehistoric Indians. Activities involving the use of flint could include the following:

1.   Children could research the physical properties that made flint so valuable to the Indian. Samples of flint could be displayed and a list made of its properties and uses.

2.   Children could write to Flint Ridge State Memorial requesting information about Flint Ridge and the methods prehistoric Indians used to mine flint. If feasible, a field trip to Flint Ridge or a similar area could be arranged.

3.   Children representing Indian flint makers could research and demonstrate authentic methods of chipping, flaking, and grinding flint, using real flint in their demonstration. Finished flint tools could be displayed in the classroom.

4.   A collector of Indian relics could be invited to display and lecture on his collection of relics and methods of hunting them.

5.   Children could search in plowed or bare fields for spearheads, arrowheads, scrapers, flint knives, and chips, all evidence of previous human existence, and bring their "finds" for examination by the class.

6.   Children could demonstrate Hopewell methods of spearmaking, showing how the spear is fastened to the shaft. Finished spears could be displayed in the classroom. Children researching spearmaking could include in their research evidence that neither the Hopewell Indians nor their predecessors used bows and arrows.

It is the mound which cries "Hopewell," assuring the Hopewell Indians permanent recognition in human history. Without the mounds and other earthworks the Hopewells might be unknown today. Geographical and topographical generalities such as the mound do not kernelize as well as man-made items. The tip of the Matterhorn, out of context, is a rock. We suggest, therefore, that such features as the mounds of the Hopewell are best re-created in three-dimensional scaled models. (See Fig. 3-4.) Be sure to provide trees or, perferably, a modern home, even if it does not belong, as a clue to the scale of the item. Suspended from the ceiling above the mound is the head of a wolf, representing the ceremonial covering of the powerful shaman or priest, leader of the "cult of the dead" burial ritual. The wolf head should be painted gray and marked with the features of the wolf. Ceremonial beads could be attached to the wolf head, symbolizing the elaborate regalia of the shaman.

The life of the Hopewell people found its highest expression and expended

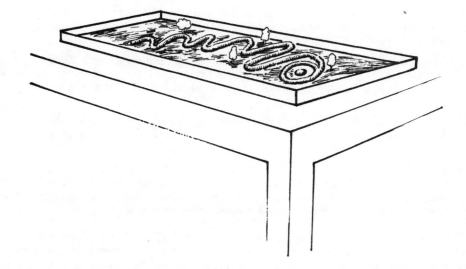

Fig. 3-4   The Kernel Design of Hopewell Mound   (James Thorpe)

its greatest efforts in meeting the mystery of death.   With complex
ceremonial rites the Hopewells marked the pathway to eternity for their
illustrious dead. Activities within this kernel design should help children to
understand and to identify with the Hopewells' preoccupation with and need
for religious expression.

1.   Children could research the dress and role of the shaman or
priest, describe the burial ritual and its importance to the Hopewell
people. A child could duplicate the shaman's ceremonial costume and
act out the role of the shaman in a make-believe burial ceremony.

2.   Hopewell persons of importance were buried with ceremonial
objects such as effigy pipes, copper breast plates, mica ornaments,
pearls, ceremonial spears, and pottery vessels.   Children   could
research these items and make facsimiles for display in the classroom
or for use in a make-believe burial ceremony.

3.   The Hopewell Indians cremated their illustrious dead in crema-
tory basins in charnel houses. After numerous cremations the charnel
houses were also burned, and the mounds were then constructed over
the sites of the charnel houses. Children could research and report on
this ritualistic procedure.

4.   The Hopewells loosened dirt for their mounds with digging sticks
and hoes of shell or bone, then carried the dirt in skins or baskets to
the sacred places where the mounds were built.   Children could
duplicate this primitive and tedious task in a corner of the schoolyard.
The entire class could be involved in the mound-building procedure,
thereby developing an appreciation for the enormity of the task and
the patience and organization required to complete the mound,
possibly stretching over many years.

5.   Children could write to the sites of the Hopewell mounds and
earthworks in Ohio requesting information in the form of brochures,
picture postcards, slides, or filmstrips. A field trip to one of the sites
could be arranged.

6.   A field trip to see the Ohio Historical Center's prehistoric Indian
display could be arranged. If this is not possible, a filmstrip of the
display could be requested.

7.   Although little evidence exists concerning the music of the
Hopewell culture, children could research and make primitive Indian
musical instruments such as drums and rattles. These instruments
could be played to a recording of authentic Indian music.

Within this total setting children can act out numerous roles simultaneously. With the Indian music in the background, the before-mentioned
activities can be brought together to form a panoramic view of primitive
Hopewell life. The flintmaker chips flint, the potter coils his clay, the
weaver works with grasses, the squaw grinds corn and tends her baby, artisans
craft an array of ceremonial objects, the shaman oversees the ceremonial
rituals of the dead. Indian food could be served. Some of the children could

become Indian traders from distant parts of North America, bringing their native products for barter. Since their languages are different, all communication would have to be by sign language or by gesturing.

Among the virtues of unifying the classroom by the kernel design method is the value of having an attractive and evocative environment remaining intact for a considerable period of time, often stimulating the relation of other short-term problems in science or mathematics to a real-life, or at least familiar, situation.

The success of the kernel design of the Hopewell Indians depends not so much on the learning of facts but on the development of appreciation for the unique contribution of the Hopewell Indians to our Ohio heritage. Such study could be considered worthwhile if the children begin to recognize the need for the perpetual preservation of these gifts of the past. It could be considered successful if one child is inspired to take to the open fields in search of yet unfound Indian relics.

The Hopewell Indians are among the ancestors of the present-day American Indians. If the Hopewell Indian lived long ago in a kind of primeval glory, how is it that the American Indian of today lives without that glory? What happened to the American Indian? To help children understand the plight of the American Indian today, spread across a corner of the classroom, as depicted in Fig. 3-5, a fence strung with rope. If feasible, real wire could be used to create the fence. Above the fence, suspended from the ceiling, a large prominently lettered sign says "Indian Reservation." No gate in the fence symbolizes the lack of communication and understanding between the Indian minority and the white majority of the United States. The fence pictures the Indian as being literally out of the American dream. This kernel design acts as a stepping stone to create awareness in the minds of children of the plight of the American Indian as a poorly represented minority group in society today.

Activities to foster this awareness could include the following:

1.   Conduct a discussion with the children concerning the effect the coming of the white man had on the Indian. Help the children to understand how the civilized white man met the Indian, altered his Stone Age culture, and then destroyed it. Ask the children whether they think this course could have been altered. Opposing sides could debate this issue.

2.   Have children research where most Indians live today.

3.   Children could become pen pals with Indian children. Ideally, this should be arranged at the beginning of the school year, so that letters have been exchanged before the study begins. Children with pen pals could tell the class what they have learned about Indian life today.

4.   Children could write to the Department of Indian Affairs in Washington, D.C. for information.

5.   Children could research and report on the Indian uprising at Wounded Knee in 1975, discovering why the Indians rebelled and what

Fig. 3-5   The Kernel Design of the Indian Today   (James Thorpe)

the final outcome was.

6.   Have the children research statistics on the average Indian standard of living versus the average white standard of living. Include information on income, education, and infant mortality.

7.   In a creative writing paper have children suggest ways Indians can improve their status. Discuss findings.

8.   Suggest that the children write a collective letter to the president asking for greater attention to Indian problems.

Much of the information necessary to complete the activities in this kernel design cannot be found in general reference works. This information is contained almost exclusively in books and brochures dealing with specific Indian sites and cultures in Ohio. Although readily available, they are often too technical to be easily understood by the average elementary-school child.
Creating suitable research material is the problem, then, and it can be

solved by preparing a series of modules for use by the children. It would be possible to furnish a research packet for each activity suggested in the kernel design. Each packet would include a cassette tape containing all important information relative to the activity being researched. This information could be given in the form of a mini-lecture by the teacher or could be a question and answer discussion between the teacher and the student. Also included in the packets would be illustrations of items referred to in the tapes or, possibly, actual items to be examined, such as flint, seeds, nuts, or roots. These packets could be checked out for study by individuals or small groups of children.

Once the design has been drafted, children can become vitally involved in filling in the details, proving through their research that the design is indeed indigenous to the Hopewell Indian culture. While the teacher anticipates certain generalizations, children prove them. They utilize the threefold technique of research - identifying ideas, analyzing them, and generalizing. In this type of learning situation, each child is able to utilize his capabililties as he is led forward by the momentum of the learning activities and his own desire to know more.

4 The Birth of a Colony: The <u>Mayflower</u> Voyage

The concept of community is basic to understanding the more global ideas of the city, state, and nation. Life aboard the <u>Mayflower</u> was a type of community existence totally foreign to most children. This chapter is included to show how children can experience the meaning of community through the kernel design approach as they role-play and research the storm-tossed 65-day voyage from Plymouth, England.

NARRATIVE STATEMENT

In the early seventeenth century, King James I did not permit freedom of religion in England but insisted that all belong to the official State Church, the Church of England. Several groups objected, but in widely differing ways. The Puritans wished to "purify" the existing church, while the separatists wanted their own denomination.

A few of the leaders among the Plymouth colonists had met, under great hardship, at the home of William Brewster for religious observances. By 1608 this proved untenable, and a number of them fled to Holland. After a short while, many of these expatriates decided the dangers of the voyage to and life in the New World were a small price to pay for retaining their native language and customs.

After an abortive beginning, during which a second ship, the <u>Speedwell</u>, proved unseaworthy, 102 passengers embarked for the New World on a historic journey. According to Bradford (1946), the hand of God was surely what saved the Puritans. One paragraph of his narrative of the voyage describes a marvelous incident:

> In sundry of these storms the winds were so fierce, and the seas so high, as they could not bear a knot of sail, but were forced to hull (lay to under shortened sail and drift with the wind) for divers days together. And in one of them as they lay at hull in a mighty storm, a lusty young man called John Howland, coming upon some occasion

above the gratings was with a roll of the ship thrown into the sea, but it pleased God that he caught hold of the topsail halliards which hung overboard and ran out at length. Yet he held his hold, though sundry fathoms under water.* (p. 94).

The trying days of continued stormy weather are made exciting in novels too. Fleming (1963), in his novel One Small Candle, describes one of the worst days:

Pandenomium now, both from men and weather. The captain and mates rushed below to gaze up from the gun deck at the sagging beam, the splintered deck around it. Water gushed through new openings, and the terrified passengers huddled against the ship's sides to escape it. The carpenter was summoned. What could be done? Nothing, unless they could force that beam back in place. The strongest men aboard - John Alden, the blasphemous boatswain's mate, and a half dozen others - put their shoulders to the job while the freezing water poured down on them. But it was like trying to raise the roof beam of a house. The massive piece of timber only sagged a little more. A spare beam was dragged up from the hold, and the men tried using that as a ram. Again, failure. Then someone remembered a "great iron screw" they had bought in Holland to help them raise houses in the New World. Maybe it would do the job. Sailors and passengers went scrambling into the hold, flinging aside boxes and bales until they found the gleam of metal in the flickering lantern light. Grunting and gasping, they lugged the screw up to the gun deck and placed it under the ruined beam. Slowly now, twist the crank, make sure the face is aimed precisely at the break, now, put your backs into it, one two three, it's going up, it's working! Ram that spare beam under it now. There!** (p. 78).

Both of these quotations help to generate a real feeling for the setting and mood, which is the primary purpose of the kernel design approach.

While the tribulations of storms are exciting, a leaky, slow ship built for freight was carrying a crew and over one hundred passengers. What makes this worthy of attention? The ship was only 100 feet long, 26 feet abeam at the widest, and with quarters for 30 crew. No passenger quarters were designed into this ship. Historians wonder still how so many persons actually lived in such crowded and hazardous conditions for 65 days. The answer, in brief, is poorly. Privacy was nonexistent. Sanitary facilities were what one

---

* William Bradford. History of Plymouth Plantation, 1606-1647. In W. T. Davis, Ed., 1946. Courtesy of BARNES & NOBLE BOOKS (Div. of Harper & Row, Publishers). Reprinted with permission.

** ONE SMALL CANDLE, by Thomas J. Fleming, W.W. Norton & Company, Inc., New York, N.Y. Copyright (C) 1963, 1964, by Thomas J. Fleming. Reprinted with permission.

might invent and probably ceased to exist entirely in poor weather. Fresh water could not be used for washing, and laundry was impossible, even in salt water. Seasickness was a daily plague. The stench of dirty bodies and casual sanitary facilities must have been overwhelming.

Food was almost a joke; most was eaten cold and often uncooked. Only occasionally did weather permit cooking fires (set in boxes of sand for some semblance of safety), and scurvy became common. The original store of fresh water soon became unpotable, probably from poor storage and the encroachment of salt water. Beer, which happily does not spoil, was the mealtime beverage for all, including small children. The hardy Puritans were also severely limited in the amount of baggage they could carry. Each family could take a Bible (in a box or loose) and one chest for all other belongings, including clothes, kitchen utensils, tools, weapons, etc. As one might guess, fear of the unknown new land resulted in many persons carrying a number of weapons at the cost of clothing.

RESEARCHING ILLUSTRATIONS

A wealth of resource material is available, both in children's literature and adult literature. Many sources contain illustrations of the ship, of the Mayflower II, an accurate reconstruction, and of section views of the interior of the ship. (See Ann McGovern, If You Sailed on the Mayflower.) Surviving narratives provide us with detailed descriptions of the persons who sailed, what they carried, and what they felt as they faced their new life. Even encyclopedia articles provide as much detail as may be needed for an overview, and illustrative material is similarly easy to locate.

KERNELIZING THE MAYFLOWER VOYAGE

Since the ship is not only described and illustrated in many sources, but still afloat as a reconstruction, it is easy to scale down the exterior or interior. The ease with which basic kernel units may be selected from photographs of the Mayflower or section views of the ship, makes the reconstruction of parts of the Mayflower in actual size fairly simple. Therefore, illustrations are not included in this chapter.

In addition to the usual cutout or mural kernel design of the ship, a sleeping cubicle or public living area may, because of its small actual size, be re-created in full scale in the classroom. Children may play act many of the exciting and difficult aspects of the journey, from crowded living conditions to food of limited quantity and quality. They may also research and perform activities in or out of the classroom which relate modern life, or familiar real-life situations to the journey of the Plymouth separatists, making the lessons learned more relevant and better remembered. Any items or artifacts which can contribute to a "nautical" atmosphere in the classroom may be used to pre-stage the actual unit of study.

SMALL-GROUP ACTIVITIES

1. The lesson plan tree, described in Chapter 2, can be used in planning unit activities that help to create the mood of the Mayflower voyage. The main branches could include the historical, religious, familial, environmental, and recreational aspects. Genealogy could be introduced in a very natural way. Even if there are no Mayflower descendents in the classroom, each student will become excited about constructing his own "family tree."

2 Construct a mural section view or "cutaway" illustration of the Mayflower.

3. Have a sailor address the class, and, with slides or illustrations, talk about a trip like that of the Mayflower.

4. Have students build a working model of a sailboat and learn about the wind and sails as motive power. Have children demonstrate what happens when they want to go one way in the sailboat and the wind blows in the opposite direction. Through the use of an electric fan, this could be easily demonstrated.

5. Invite several other classes in your school to help you put 102 persons, the number on the Mayflower voyage, in your classroom for a substantial period. Tape the noise and videotape the crowded conditions. This should lead to a real feeling for the crowded conditions experienced by the people on the Mayflower. Another alternative to this would be to section off the classroom, using one-third of the average classroom. Discuss the effects of such crowding. Have the children take a rest or nap under these circumstances.

6. Taste salt water. Wash hands and face with it for a day.

7. Collect a typical Puritan family's belongings and store these in a box. Compare this box with what your family owns and would carry if they moved.

8. Make a Mayflower meal of salt pork, hard tack, and a warm flat root beer. (Substitute for beer)

9. From your "family's" box of belongings select tools and implements and discover how to survive. How could these few tools be used? What else would be needed?

10. Take any type of an object in the classroom, and have students brainstorm the possible uses of the object if they were stranded on an island.

11. Plan a journey of equal distance to that of the Mayflower voyage. Pretend each child's family will make that move. Have them list what will be moved, how it will be carried, how long the trip will take, and what will be done on arrival of the destination. Compare with the Mayflower voyage.

SUMMARY

The present is influenced and, to varying degrees, shaped by the past. One of the less obvious virtues of a unit of study as narrowly defined as this one is its value as an introduction to other units. For example, what could be more logical for a pioneer unit than a reconstruction of the Plymouth Colony and a period of living under the Mayflower Compact, meeting and getting to know Indians and discovering the real meaning of Thanksgiving? If teachers help students to see these relationships of the past to subsequent events, students will gain a more realistic historical perspective. If the school district's social studies curriculum follows a chronological sequence, appropriate segments of the kernel designs could be retained during the transition into the next unit. This would help students unify concepts of the various disciplines in an understanding of society and social life. Furthermore, it would help students to apply various historical frames of reference to the study of human life and its current environment.

REFERENCES

Bradford, W.   History of Plymouth plantation, 1606-1647, edited by W. T. Davis. New York: Barnes & Noble, 1946.
Fleming, T. One small candle. New York: Norton, 1963.
McGovern, A. If you sailed on the Mayflower. New York: Scholastic Book Service, 1970.

5 A Kernel Design Related to Statehood: Ohio's Buckeye Frontier

Most state education departments require a study of one's respective state. This kernel design of Ohio's frontier is included to illustrate how teachers can use this creative concept to help children understand better the development of their own state from unspoiled wilderness to its present condition.

Interacting with the kernel design, children will discover answers to such questions as:

Who were these people who settled in the territory from which their respective state was carved?

From where did they come?

How did they come?

Why did they come?

What ideals, hopes, and fears did they bring with them?

How did they solve the everyday problems of existing in the unsettled lands?

What was the attraction of the untamed wilderness that took men from their homes and even families to endure hardship never before experienced?

NARRATIVE STATEMENT

Frontier America was diverse, covering several fairly well-defined historical periods, and progressing from one geography to another. What made pioneers of some men and their families, while others remained behind? What was the attraction of the untamed western wilderness that took men from their homes or even from their families to move west and to endure hardship never before experienced or dreamed? Land! Free virgin land, as much of it as a person could ever want for his own. Beginning with our Puritan progenitors, Americans have been typified by a strong drive for total self-sufficiency, for a freedom of expression which even extended at times to an abhorrence for physical boundaries.

The early pioneers found Ohio a paradise of sorts. There were virgin forests of nearly every type of tree - maple, hickory, oak, ash, walnut - all the native woods needed by a self-sufficient craftsman to produce shelter, tools, and utensils for his family. There was ample water, with many streams of significant size for both table water and transport, and an annual rainfall in excess of 30 inches. The forests were full of game, the streams full of fish, and the Indians not normally hostile. All a man had to do to build a house was fell enough trees to clear space for a house and a barn and use the ready-made building material thus provided. This was not the life for everyone, for it was never easy, but it is small wonder that the hardier persons needing freedom and space soon built homes and villages in Ohio.

The first documented settlement in Ohio was Schoenbrunn, near the present city of New Philadelphia. The population was mixed, with a group of Moravian missionaries dedicated to bringing Christianity to the "heathen" and about 250 Christian Indians living together there for some years. Schoenbrunn was later abandoned and the first permanent settlement was built around a fort called Campus Maritus. After 1775 and the treaty of Greenville, Indian attacks were rare and the fort was abandoned.

The first lasting settlement of the newly created Western Reserve was Marietta. Cincinnati soon followed, growing at a greater rate, for it was the Ohio River which took many pioneer families even farther west. The Ohio River (La Belle Reviere to the French explorers) may have derived its name, like those of many early settlements, from the Iroquois, in this case "O-hey-yo," or "great river." Between Cleveland and Cincinnati many small settlements soon grew. These were small communities of hardy backwoods-men who typified the American pioneer spirit.

The first pioneers to follow the early explorers were "squatters," many of Scotch-Irish descent. These were followed by New England Puritans, English Quakers, Dutch Religionists (Lutherans, Reformed, Dunkards) from Pennsylvania, Scotch-Irish Presbyterians, and French Huguenot descendants. Many came directly from England or Europe. It is little wonder that for many years the church was the social center of the Ohio settlement and revivals were a popular entertainment form. The church, for example, was the first building erected by David Zeisberger at Schoenbrunn in 1722.

RESEARCHING ILLUSTRATIONS

A wealth of illustrative material may be found for this kernel design. Photographs of extant buildings and settlements are available. Simplified, generalized paintings, drawings, or sketches, as well as illustrated children's literature books are plentiful. Chambers of Commerce and travel agencies have valuable resource material.

KERNELIZING THE UNIQUENESS OF THE BUCKEYE FRONTIER

Of all the possible creative environments for social studies subjects, pioneer heritage is one of the most important and easiest to design. The exterior simplicity of the architecture, social structure, or economic structure of a frontier settlement makes it an ideal subject for a kernel design. Further, the pioneers and Indians are already familiar to children through the cinema, television, and books, and are therefore easy to role-play.

To re-create an early settlement one could begin with a log house and then add other important elements of a typical community: the church, a school, a general store, a blacksmith shop, and perhaps a mill. Since the log cabin and other aspects of primitive or early settlement communities may be found all across America and used in many different ways to support a learning experience in community, we have elected to illustrate in more complete fashion the technique of kernelizing these buildings in Chapter 12. There you will find a discussion of design simplification and some helpful hints on manipulating different materials to fashion evocative and economical colonial representations.

SMALL-GROUP ACTIVITIES

Re-creating an early settlement in the classroom provides a variety of research subjects for completing the creative environment. To further illustrate the interdisciplinary planning wheel described in Chapter 2, activities have been designed around the social science disciplines. (See Fig. 5-1.)

Sample activities related to geography

1.   Make maps indicating the land grants, the roads cut into the territory, the location of the Northwestern Territory, and the locations of the early settlements.

2.   Collect illustrations of trees, plants, and animals found by the early settlers.

Sample activities related to sociology and anthropology

1.   Learn typical dances such as the minuet and the Virginia Reel.

2.   Have children role-play or write a play about life in the frontier.

3.   The Moravians were often called the most musical people in our country between 1750 and 1850. Their music dealt almost entirely with the central thing of importance in their lives - their faith. Have children research Moravian hymns, which were based primarily on the psalms.

4. To help students realize how difficult it was for families to pack up and go west to the Ohio country, role-play a current family scene in which father comes home today and discusses the need to move to a distant state. The reactions of the teen-agers, the star football player of the family, the married child, the mother, the grandparents, might be enacted and discussed.

5. There was little time for recreation in the pioneer days. Fun was gained through activities related to work. Research ways in which people entertained themselves.

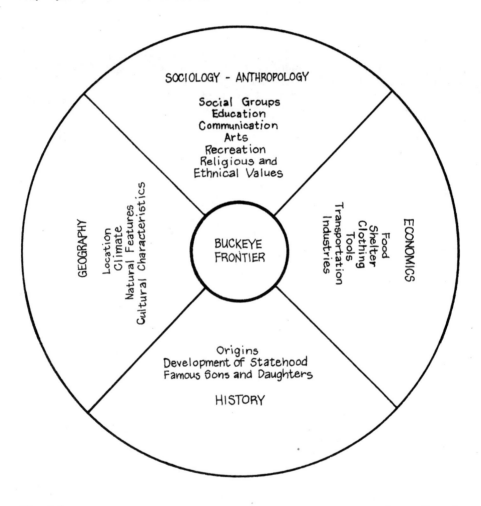

Fig. 5-1   Interdisciplinary Planning Wheel for Unit on Buckeye Frontier
(James Thorpe)

Sample activities related to economics

1. Dyes can be made from plants in the area.

2. A loom or spinning wheel demonstration might be given by a local craftsperson.

3. Students can assume the role of costume designers as part of the learning experience. After researching the thematic time period, they could design various types of clothing. Old, dyed sheets can be used for special effects in costuming, as well as the use of clothing children already have. Basic clothes can be altered with crepe paper, pieces of material, or paper designs; jewelry, hats, wigs, purses, and scarves can often give a sense of authenticity to the character.

4. A kernelized log cabin can be constructed using rug rolls. (See Chapter 12 for detailed directions.) Cracks could be chinked with chips and a mixture of clay and moss. In order to add to the authenticity of the log cabin, the following questions could be researched, discussed, and added to the kernel design:

.   How was the interior of the cabin divided?

.   What activities were carried on within the pioneer's cabin that are not common today?

.   How did the pioneers light their cabins?

.   Because of housing and living conditions, do you think the pioneers thought of themselves as being poor?

.   What methods did the pioneers use to clear the land? Who did this work? What tools were used?

.   Did the clearing of the land frequently involve the help of others? How did the pioneers pay for this outside help? Did money play an important role in clearing the land? Why or why not?

.   How did pioneer families manage to survive between the time they arrived in the Ohio country and the time they built their shelters?

.   In what way did the Ohio pioneer's view of his environment resemble or differ from that of the Delaware Indians? How did their houses differ?

.   What kind of furniture did the frontier family have? Was their furniture purchased or made? What materials were used in making the furniture? Were aesthetic qualities important in furnishing a pioneer home?

.   What utensils were commonly found in a pioneer's house? Were the utensils purchased or made? What materials were used in making his utensils? Where were they obtained? Who made the utensils?

.   What household items were highly valued by the pioneer family?

5.   A fort with blockhouses might be kernelized or modeled.

6.   Small gardens could be started, showing the crops that were grown by the settlers.

7.   Wool, flax, and cotton could be acquired from farms in some areas. These could be cleaned, carded, dyed, and spun into yarn.

8.   A meal using only foods available to the frontier people could be prepared, using primitive means of cooking.

9.   Research ways of food preservation, such as drying, salting, and pickling.

10.   Make puppets to illustrate the clothing of the period.

11.   Model or kernelize a covered wagon or flatboat.

Sample activities related to historical developments

1.   Invite the curator from a local museum to speak on artifacts from the area.

2.   Have students write imaginative diaries or logs of people who lived during the time of the early settlement of Ohio or have children locate in the library copies of original narratives.

3.   A weekly "Buckeye Frontier Newspaper" might be published.

4.   Have students write their own genealogies or histories of their national origins.

5.   Plan study tours to some local historical sites.

We have often referred to the ease with which many creative atmospheres or activities may be researched and to the wealth of information and illustrative material available in the most common of sources. While study tours in Ohio will be of limited value to teachers from other areas, we have listed, from brochures published by various chambers of commerce, the following tours, simply as a practical example of this very simple research process. Even though study tours to all these places could be economically impossible, small groups of students could research the various places and pretend that they are tourist guides taking the other members of the class on a "guided simulated tour." Older students might construct their own kernel designs appropriate for the "guided tour." Examples of historical sites in Ohio include the following:

New Philadelphia area - Zoar Village, Schoenbrunn (first Ohio village - 1772; Gnadenhutten (place of Indian mission and massacre of 1782); Trumpet in the Land (outdoor drama of the first Ohio settlement); Fort Laurens - (Ohio's only Revolutionary War fort); Lebanon - Golden Lamb

Inn (Ohio's oldest inn - 1803); Metal Park - largest geodesic dome in the United States; Akron - Railways of America Museum; Burton - Burton Pioneer Village (typical Western Reserve community); West Liberty - Piatt Castles; Dayton - Air and Space Museum; Marietta area - Campus Maritus, Putnam House, Ohio River Museum, Ohio Land Office (Ohio's oldest building); Chillicothe (Ohio's first capital) -Ross County Museum; Gazette (oldest newspaper west of the Alleghenies); Columbus - Ohio Historical Center, restored German village; Miami University, Oxford - McGuffy House; Norwich - Zane Grey Museum, National Road Museum; Coshocton - Roscoe village restoration; Mt. Pleasant - Betty Zane Memorial; Roseville - Ohio Ceramic Center; Gallipolis - third permanent settlement; Fort Ancient - America's largest prehistoric fort; Norwalk - Firelands Historical.

6.   We are the reflection of our founding fathers; we have been influenced by their strength and courage.   An appreciation of American growth from the time of the Buckeye frontier to today's technological society can be gained by further research and instructional activities related to the following historical areas:

Ohio Indians

Tribes

Characteristics

Joining with the white man

Missionary influence (Schoenbrunn and Gnadenhutten)

Type of houses

Holidays and ceremonies

Influence on the white man

Development of statehood

Marietta Code

State constitutions (1802, 1851, 1912)

People who helped bring about statehood

Forms of government

Development of industries

Agriculture

Steel

Pottery

Rubber

Coal (strip mining versus shafts)

Shipping

Electrical and nuclear power

<u>Ecology in the state</u>

"Death" of Lake Erie

Flood controls

Waste of natural resources

Current conservation efforts

<u>Famous sons and daughters of Ohio</u>

Military

Education

Inventors

Political (presidents, first ladies, vice-presidents, senators, justices of the Supreme Court)

Pioneers

<u>Developments in modes of travel and their effect upon the state</u>

Railroads

Modern highways

Airplane and lighter-than-air machines

Canals and waterways

SUMMARY

By reconstructing the lifestyles of the people in Ohio before automation, electricity, and modern transportation, students will discover both the hard times on the frontier and the manner in which the pioneers responded. Role-playing and researching life in the wilderness will probably lead students to a greater appreciation of the pioneer's use of problem-solving skills, ingenuity, and labor in developing their homes and communities; to an appreciation of their ability to work with other members of the family and community; to a sense of responsibility toward one another; and to one of the greatest joys of all, a feeling of accomplishment.

6 A Kernel Design of Hawaii

This kernel design has been included to illustrate a study of a place and a culture with fewer unique aspects than some others we have suggested. Palm trees are as common to Florida and California as they are to Hawaii. To kernelize Hawaii, it is necessary to develop activities that are related to historical or anthropological aspects of the area.

NARRATIVE STATEMENT

The Hawaiian Islands today are a mélange of cultures - Polynesian, European, Chinese, Japanese and American. The first settlers, the Polynesians, brought from Tahiti and Nuku Hiva many of the food crops now thought to be typical of Hawaii; the Orientals brought industriousness, farming and commerce; Europe gave its political follies; and America brought Christianity, law, and disease.

It is thought that the islands were first settled about 750 A.D., but the full fruition of the Hawaiian tradition was not reached until the mid-nineteenth century, when the Polynesian culture had been thoroughly diluted by many others. James Cook visited the islands in January of 1778, but not until about 1820 were the islanders exposed to other cultures in depth, as a result of the arrival of the colonist missionaries from America. There are several schools of thought, often diametrically opposed, on the value of the contributions of these ascetic fundamentalists.

We have successfully used a very brief chronological chart or outline in composing narrative statements for social studies units like this. Our kernel design of England (See Chapter 7) is simplified immeasurably by such an outline, for it provides not only a chronology but a stylistic frame of reference as well. Such a table may be of considerable length of detail, or it may be as simple as the one included here. The table may be done as a decorative poster or bulletin board and used as another constant reminder of the scope of the study unit.

Hawaii's history may be broken down into four parts:

1.   Genesis - from the Stone Age Polynesians through the emigration north to Hawaii;

2.   First look at the world - from Captain Cook (1778) to the missionaries (1820);

3.   Invasion and occupation - the missionaries to Liliuokalani, the last of the monarchs;

4.   Provisional government - Stanford Dole (1893) to the present.

Novels may often be overlooked as good sources of information, or just as a place for your class to start researching for a creative atmosphere design. While many novels are of absolutely no value for research purposes, others, such as Robert Louis Stevenson's Travels in Hawaii (1973) or James Michener's Hawaii (1959) incorporate much predigested history. Stevenson's book is of special value, as it can easily be read by students ten years of age or older. In fact, the virtue of the novel, or of fictionalized history is that it is predigested - made easier and more enjoyable to read. Stevenson's descriptive literary style in picturing Hawaii can catch the interest very well:

Corrugated slopes of lava, bristling lava cliffs, sprouts of metallic clinkers, miles of coast without a well or rivulet, scarce anywhere a beach, nowhere a harbor - here seems a singular land to be contended for in battle as a seat for courts and princes. Yet it possessed in the eyes of the natives a more than countervailing advantage. The windward shores of the isle are beaten by a monstrous surf; there are places where goods and passengers must be hauled up and lowered by a rope; there are coves which even the daring boatmen of Hamakua dread to enter; and men live isolated in their hamlets or communicate by giddy footpaths in the cliff. Upon the side of Kona the tablelike margin of the lava affords almost everywhere a passage by land, and the waves, reduced by the vast breakwater of the island, allow an almost continual communication by way of sea. Yet even here the surf of the Pacific appears formidable to the stranger as he lands, and daily delights him with its beauty as he walks the shore.* (p. 7)

Hawaii today is primarily a tourist attraction to the rest of the world, although some of the attributes of paradise accorded the islands have been displaced by progress or confused with those of Tahiti and Bora Bora. The "crossroads of the Pacific" does have, however, an almost perfect climate and a vital, kaleidoscopically varying social presence.

The language of the island is among the most pleasing and musical in the world. Most words end on a vowel, with the accent usually on the penultimate, so that they are almost sung when properly pronounced. Since some school libraries may not contain Hawaiian dictionaries, we have included a simplified set of rules for pronunciation, from which your class can begin to properly pronounce the Hawaiian words they will encounter in their

---

* Robert Lewis Stevenson, Travels in Hawaii, A. Grove Day, ed. Honolulu: The University Press of Hawaii, 1973. Reprinted with permission.

initial research and reading on Hawaii.

Rule 1:   Accent on the penultimate.

Rule 2:   Accent in two-syllable words on the first syllable, except when the second of the two syllables has been dipthongized. Then the accent is on the first part of the dipthong (for instance, the word makai is pronounced ma - ka - i).

Rule 3:   Vowels are pronounced: a as in above; e as in weigh; i as in marine; o as in no; u as in true; w often pronounced as v.

These rules are not a suitable substitute for a dictionary of pronunciation; rather, they are included as an example of the simplicity of the early steps in kernelizing any foreign culture. The rules of pronunciation for Italian, for example, may be simplified in much the same way to heighten interest in discussion and reading on Italy as a new place or culture.

Pidgin English is the second official language of the islands, and is the common casual language of the uneducated islander, though it is often heard as well on the campus of the University of Hawaii. Pidgin may be pronounced as if English, but softened and blurred. (For example, "What's the matter?" is sounded "wassamadda?"). Terms are compressed (for example, "a waste of time" becomes "wasetime" or "go slowly so I can catch up with you later" becomes "go-stay-go," or "my brother is asleep" becomes "mu brudda sleep"). An essential expression in Pidgin is "da kine" ("that kind" or "that way") and the expression may be, in context, as vague or as explicit as the speaker wishes, (for example, "da kine about her" means "that way about" or "in love with her").

The cuisine of Hawaii today is essentially American, but with Hawaiian, French, and Oriental overtones. The classic meal is the luau, in which roast pig is the main dish, cooked with sweet potatoes, plantains, butterfish, and taro shoots wrapped in ti leaves and seasoned finally with salt and shoyu sauce. Another classic, not a favorite of Americans though, is poi, a thick purplish starch paste made from taro root and eaten with the fingers. Hawaiians are also lovers and consummate cooks of all manner of seafood, often prepared with fruit or coconut meat or milk. It is interesting to note that true Hawaiian food has changed little with the passing of over 1,000 years. One aspect is somewhat altered though; men no longer must cook certain kapu foods, such as coconuts, bananas, and most fish, that could not be prepared by women. One wonders if this is the reason the islanders ate so many cold, uncooked meals.

RESEARCHING ILLUSTRATIONS

Four basic types of literature were used to locate illustrations for this example of the creative classroom environment: encyclopedias, histories, guide books, and children's books. Many photographs, etchings, and drawings may be found, but most picture an atmosphere difficult to kernelize. They do create, however, a general feeling of Hawaii. Since much of the illustrated material truly evocative of Hawaii is either of anthropological or costume nature, these illustrations can be used to help children design their own Hawaiian costumes to wear during the study of Hawaii. Contrasting costumes can be made showing the red and yellow feather cloak, helmet, the tapa loin cloth of the noble ancestors, and the modern "sarong" usually affected for the benefit of tourists.

The numerous illustrations will lead children to discover that the Hawaii of today represents a contrast in architecture, such as represented in Fig. 6-1.

On the left of Fig. 6-1 is a reconstruction of a royal pavilion, made of grass. This pavilion was once the royal palace at Kailua, on the Kona coast of Hawaii. On the right is a more modern, but typical Hawaiian amalgamation of eastern and western styles, exemplified by this Chinese Christian church. Remember that, whatever the source in illustrative material, one of the most important clues to Hawaii is color. Vivid, contrasting, almost overwhelming color is one of the first things noticed by visitors to the islands.

KERNELIZING HAWAII

Part of the kernelizing process is the design of activities, for, as in this example, it is clear that the scenic elements alone will not be unmistakably Hawaiian. It is what is under the skeleton palm or in the cutaway grass shack that helps the student to generalize.

Basic scenic elements for this creative atmosphere could include the coconut palm, the grass pavilion, the lei, and the grass skirt or "sarong" of brilliant cloth. Each of these can be, with minimal teacher assistance, child-produced of paper or cardboard. Further, these elements are the common elements of illustrations found in a number of children's books so that even the basic designs may be child-produced.

The lei and the grass skirt, the cape of feathers, the muumuu or the malo, worn in a setting of palms and sand, will be sufficient to make your Hawaii. Combined with the costumes, kernelized history in statuary (such as the famous 100-foot war canoe or the "typical" grass house, pavilion, or shack) easily creates the islands in the classroom. One of the secrets of re-creating Hawaii lies in strong, vibrant colors. The blue of the Pacific, the many greens of foliage, the kaleidoscope of flowers, and the brilliant cloth of the muumuu make most other spots of scenic beauty look bland and faded.

Dance and music are more than cultural in Hawaii; they are scenic. The hula, either Tahitian or Hawaiian, is a beautiful dance, created according to legend to amuse the fire goddess, Pele. Accompanied by the "slack-string" guitar, the hula is the island's chief contribution to the world of entertainment, and no single scene is so evocative of Hawaiian or Polynesian culture as white sand, swaying palms, slack-string guitar, and the exquisite grace of the hula, performed by men and children with the same beauty and expression as the island women.

The hula is not easy to learn, for the vocabulary of the hands is surprisingly large. The body plays only a small part in the storytelling of the hula, but the coordination of moving feet, undulating hips and torso, and expressive hands and arms is quite difficult. Nevertheless, some attempt should be made by the children at this most graceful of all dances. Bare feet

Fig. 6-1 A Contrast in Architecture   (Jon Cobes)

and light, loose clothing, should be available during the dance.

Sample activities that would help children live "Hawaii" include the following:

1.   Lunch time could become a luau, a meal on the floor. Each child could contribute to a potluck or just bring a snack lunch. Mats could be woven of crepe paper or paper-bag strips and serve as the "tablecloth" to hold the food. Simple drums and instruments could be made 'for performing at the luau.

2.   Polynesian myths and stories could be told and new ones created. These stories were handed down orally from generation to generation. This activity would give the children a better understanding of folk tales and their origins.

3.   Learn to use the Hawaiian language.   The class might study Hawaiian words for a period of each day to create songs, stories, and poetry.

4.   Plant a garden of tropical plants, using only a digging stick. After enjoying the sweet meat of a pineapple, the children could plant the top and watch it grow.

5.   Drawing or making boats would open up an interest in the world of the sea.   The children could see the differences in construction and uses between the boats of the Polynesians and the Europeans.

6.   Try studying and learning in the old way for a brief period each day. The children might sit on the floor while the teacher defines a Hawaiian word and then the children repeat the word in unison.

7.   Designing tourist centers will get the class involved in the geographical and historical features of Hawaii. By planning "sight-seeing tours," the children can in effect present reports on Hawaii.

8.   Write a constitution for the classroom.   This period of Hawaii's history parallels the time when a standardized form of government came into existence for the islanders.   By designing, voting on, obeying, and revising the laws of the constitution, the class would begin to understand how a democracy works.

9.   Make a "Monopoly"-like game about the success of a plantation and businesses of other sorts. The chance cards might read like this: "No rain for six weeks, pineapple crop fails, pay $1,000" or "Gold Rush in California creates demand for Hawaiian goods, collect $250 from bank." This could be fun and a challenge to the children. They would begin to wonder about these facts, and, if suitable reference materials are available, would begin to read about them. The children could also be challenged to make up chance cards related to researched facts about Hawaii.

10. Have children research types of Hawaiian sports and contrast them to the sports of the Unted States.

11. With background music, have children pretend through movement that they are palm trees swaying in the breeze of the ocean in calm and in storm.

SUMMARY

The study of Hawaii can and should be very enriching for the children. The things that they learn from this study can be carried over into the study of any area of the world. Hawaii is usually a romantic place in our minds, but it is also a real place to study and enjoy.

REFERENCE

Stevenson, Robert Lewis. Travels in Hawaii. Honolulu: University Press of Hawaii, 1973.

SUPPLEMENTARY BIBLIOGRAPHY

Fodor, E., and Curtis, W., eds. Fodor's guide to Hawaii. New York: McKay, 1968.

Kuykendall, R. S. The Hawaiian kingdom: 1874-1893. Honolulu: University Press of Hawaii, 1967.

Michener, James A. Hawaii. New York: Random House, 1959.

Pierce, N. R. The Pacific states of America. New York: Norton, 1972.

Pratt, J. W. Expansionists of 1898: The acquisition of Hawaii and the Spanish islands. Gloucester, Mass.: Peter Smith, 1959.

7 A Kernel Design of the History of England Through Architecture

The obvious limitations of this chapter title in no way reduce the effectiveness of such a study. To attempt to re-create and live the history of an empire such as Britain, now in its second millennium, would be sheerest futility.

A careless overview may result in the idea of England simply as the mother country to the United States and of English as the mother tongue. It is instructive, though, to note that England herself is a mélange of European cultures and her language a construct resulting from many centuries of occupation or influence. Americans are also the result of centuries of blending of dozens of cultures. America was truly a "melting pot of nationalities" many years before immigrants began to swell our modern urban centers. In order to understand and appreciate the historical roots of our own American culture, major social studies curriculums include a comprehensive unit on England.

At the risk of oversimplification, the long and colorful history of England is seen most clearly on an elementary level when divided into four areas -art and architecture, customs and traditions, politics and government, and energy and transportation. An in-depth study of England will, of course, provide that these areas of concern are inextricably intertwined but, for purposes of introductory study, it is possible to consider each as an entity. Customs and traditions might initially appear the easiest and most profitable area, especially for younger children, but no area so clearly and graphically defines and limits the periods of development of the British heritage as does its architecture. By looking at British architecture in six broadly defined periods, this chapter shows how other important developmental concerns such as customs and traditions may more easily be placed in perspective and chronology.

NARRATIVE STATEMENT

Period British architecture may be viewed in terms of Saxon influence,

Norman influence, the Gothic period, the Tudor period, the Baroque period, and the Georgian period. This simplified division covers a period of time from about the fifth century A.D. to the mid-nineteenth century. Many fine original examples or revivals of the buildings of each period still stand in England, and, interestingly, many fine revivals of buildings from most of these periods may be visited in the United States.

The British architectural periods following the departure of the Romans in A.D. 410 as outlined by Fletcher (1963) are condensed in Table 1. His classification is based on Rickman's division of English sovereigns and on that of Sharpe, whose periods are determined by the evolution of window tracery.

Table1. Architectural periods of England and their style names

Dates (A.D.)	Periods	Style Names
449-1066	5th to 11th centuries	Anglo-Saxon
1066-1189	Part of the 11th century through the 12th century	Norman
1189-1307	13th century	Early English (Lancet)
1307-1377	14th century	Decorated Gothic (Geometrical Curvilinear)
1377-1485	15th century	Perpendicular Gothic (Rectilinear)
1485-1558	First half of the 16th century	Tudor
1690-1750	First half of the 18th century	Baroque
1714-1830	Reign of Kings George	Georgian

Although each period is reasonably defined, the transition from one style to another was gradual and is often difficult to trace. Furthermore, these somewhat arbitrary style names cannot be considered scientific, as they are based partly on historical periods and partly on architectural character; but, as they have been commonly applied for so long to all descriptions of English architecture, they have become an accepted part of architectural phraseology. They refer approximately to the type of architecture prevalent during the centuries with which they are identified. Architectural details in various museums correspond with these style names.

Saxon influence

The Saxons invaded and conquered the British Isles in the late fifth century A.D.   British and Roman elements of architecture were tempered by a strong German influence from that time until A.D. 1066 (the time of William the Conqueror). The result was a severe architecture, tending to tall, narrow structures, instead of the low, rambling interconnected buildings of medieval Italy, for example. Even in this restrained architecture, there are strong Roman influences seen in repeated low round arches and arched slit windows. It is instructive to note that, while most surviving examples of Anglo-Saxon architecture are churches, a few domiciles remain to show the contrast in attention to detail. Compared to the church, the typical domicile was a poor thing indeed.

Norman influence

England had been aware of continental European trends, we are sure, prior to the arrival of William the Conqueror in 1066, but from this date on for about the next hundred years, the predominate influence was that of Normandy. Buildings became less tall and severe, more bold and massive. They were typified by a stronger Roman influence. There were more openings in round, Romanesque arches; recessed arched windows; and, for the first time, carvings, both in stone and in wood, were used for decorative purposes.

Gothic architecture

After William and the Norman influence, some trade and general travel brought knowledge of the emergence of Gothic architecture to England. A logical outgrowth of the Romanesque, Gothic architecture became typified by soaring heights, arches on slender pillars now pointed instead of round (a physical, or structural, necessity as well as a decorative invention), stained glass, ribbed vaults, and a profusion of carvings, mainly in oak. The ogee arch and pierced stone tracery appeared. Decorative wood carving, in general, dates from the Gothic period. It was natural that Britain embraced this new architecture, especially its churches and monumenal buildings, for its beauty remains unsurpassed today.   Again, note that churches and monumental buildings - castles, palaces - received the major benefit of attention to architectural innovation. Most domiciles in the Gothic period (and even after) retained of a humble, restrained appearance, strongly reminiscent of the Saxon and Norman periods.

Tudor architecture

Named for its development during the reign of the Tudor family, this architectural "style" is actually many developmental steps, from the perpendicular Gothic of churches culminating in the "Elizabethan" half-timbered domicile of Shakespeare's time. Tudor architecture, with its lavish heraldic carving, gables, and high molded chimneys, is mainly seen in homes. The Renaissance architecture of Europe is seen in later churches and monumental buildings and is strongly influenced by both church Gothic and Renaissance. Typical are more rounded arches, shallow decorative carving, much stained glass, and extensive paneling. The Gothic influence on more pretentious homes is seen in the great hall, often more than two stories high, with open beams resembling the ceiling of a cathedral.

Baroque architecture

Evident in England from 1690 to 1750, Baroque architecture was an outgrowth of the Renaissance. It was typified in interior design with extensive ornamentation and strongly curved lines everywhere. The round arch almost completely supplanted the Gothic arch and many examples of the post and lintel doorway or window, typical of the classical revival of the Renaissance, are seen. By comparison with the Gothic, The English Baroque was severe and rectilinear, on the outside at least.

Georgian architecture

Typifying the reigns of the four Kings George, from 1714 to 1830, Georgian architecture retained only a slight influence of the Gothic, but it is more a true classic revival than early Renaissance. The arched door or window was nearly gone, and was replaced by the classic pediment, often broken at the center and finished with a finial. An occasional arched pediment was a reminder of the Roman and Gothic. Pillars and pilasters, with classic fluting and decoration were further classical echoes, both inside and outside. Shallow carved moldings and extensive, if severe, paneling also echo Tudor and "Elizabethan" homes.

A brief social chronology of Britain is included here as an example of how the narrative statement can help to generate relevant classroom research activities that can be role-played or reenacted within the kernel design.

Table 2. Social chronology of England

Roman Period

55 and 54 B.C.	Julius Caesar landed in Britain.
43 A.D.	The Roman conquest of Britain actually began.
77-210	The Walls of Hadrian and Antoninus Pius were built.
410	Much of the Roman work was destroyed by invading Saxons and Jutes.

Anglo-Saxon Period

450-600	The Saxons and Jutes settled. Arthurian legends appeared to describe these invaders.
600	Saxons were largely Christianized.
865	First invasion by the Danes occurred.
1042	Cnute, a Dane, became King of England.
1066-1754	The feudal system was introduced to Britain.

Norman Period
1154-1399   Castles were built with towns surrounding as trading
                             centers.

Plantagenet Period
1320   Norman and British cultures were firmly combined.
1344-1400   Schools, such as Oxford and Cambridge, were organized
                             in recognizable form.
                             Chaucer.
c. 1350-1400   English language replaced French at court.
c. 1380   Science of heraldry developed. This had a strong
                             influence on architectural ornamentation.
1399-1485   Wars of the Roses occurred.

Lancastrian and Yorkist Period
1455-1558   Introduction and development of printing occurred in
                             England.
                             More schools and colleges were founded.
                             Lancaster and York were united.

Tudor Period
1515-1550   Clergy declined in importance.
                             Domestic architecture became important for the first
                             time.
                             Tudor   architecture   was   developed   for   country
                             gentlemen.
                             Sir Thomas Moore.
                             Full fruition of Gothic architecture as Tudor was
                             reached.

RESEARCHING ILLUSTRATIONS

There is a wealth of illustrative material in encyclopedias and tourist
guides easily available to any researcher. However, most of the illustrations
are simply repeated from volume to volume. For example, the number of
Anglo-Saxon buildings still standing today is very small. Thus nearly any
pictorial history of western architecture will supply all the illustrations you
will need.

KERNELIZING THE ARCHITECTURAL PERIODS OF ENGLAND

The classroom could be sectioned into six areas to depict the six
architectural periods summarized in the narrative statement.   Cardboard
frameworks, as shown in Figs. 7-1 to 7-5, can be enlarged and extended from
the ceiling or attached to the wall. The class, likewise, could be divided into
six groups. Each group could research the architecture indigenous to the
specific historical period and finish the numerous details on each of the
cardboard kernel designs.

Fig. 7-1 Saxon Architecture. 540 Earl's Barton Church, Northamptonshire.
Tenth Century.   This is perhaps the finest example of Anglo-Saxon
architecture that has come down to us. It has been suggested that the
pilaster strips on the surface derive from wooden prototypes.   (Jon Cobes)

Saxon architecture

Saxon architecture may be quite difficult to kernelize, for there are few examples from which to choose. Many buildings, as the one chosen here, have design elements at once distinctive and predating later periods. The ogee-arched windows in this example, out of context, might be confused with some examples of Gothic. The series of arches supported by squat pillars and topped by the crenelated "battlement" make a distinctive kernel design which can be suspended or even taped or tacked to a wall.

Norman architecture

This example of Norman architecture is often observed as the "crusader's castle," which it resembled in many particulars. Unlike Saxon buildings,

Fig. 7-2   Norman Architecture   (Jon Cobes)

Norman architecture commonly had round towers. A more unique aspect is found at the top of the square central tower, in the corbeled, or machicolated battlement. Corbeling (a series of masonry or brick courses, each built out beyond the one below it, to support a chimney, oriel window, turret, etc.) became rather common in later styles, but it was unusual at this time. This is an easy kernel design, whether two- or three-dimensional, and it is one which many children will recognize immediately.

Gothic architecture

Gothic, in its classic examples, provides many distinctive details. To avoid confusion when single details, out of context, may look like Tudor or Elizabethan, or even echo the Saxon or Norman styles, interior detail can be used for this kernel design. The soaring vaulted ceilings, the magnificent windows, or even the profusion of carved symbols all evoke the church or cathedral, and thus the "Gothic" to most people. An interesting and potentially exquisite classroom decor would be a child-researched and produced "stained glass" window made of cardboard or light wood and theatrical gelatin. Few other design elements, however distinctive, can so easily evoke the desired image of size and grandeur so typical of Gothic architecture as the stained glass window. (See Chapter 12 for detailed directions on modifying the classroom windows and doorway to create distinctive architectural kernel designs.)

Tudor architecture

Tudor, or more properly in this fine example, Elizabethan half-timbered buildings, have many striking and unique details. The most obvious is the flattened, two-centered Tudor arch, often decorated with the Tudor flower (a trefoil-like device) or a repeated quatrefoil. This illustration shows these details as separate, but they may be effectively combined. The danger in this combination is in not completing sufficient additional detail to distinguish the kernel design from certain examples of architecture from earlier periods.

Baroque architecture

English Baroque is a style used for only a generation or two. Thus few classic examples are found outside the work of Christopher Wren and his disciples. Further – and this may be true of all kernels of architectural detail or development - interior and exterior detail are often strikingly different. This fine example, however, provides a few details common to both interior and exterior Baroque design, in the simple Romanesque arch topped by garlanding. This combination will even be commonly observed as fireplace decor.

Fig. 7-3 Tudor Architecture (Jon Cobes)

Fig. 7-4 Baroque Architecture (Jon Cobes)

Fig. 7-5 Georgian Architecture (Jon Cobes)

Georgian architecture

Similar in so many ways to the better examples of Baroque architecture, the early Georgian illustrates well the difficulty of drawing a line between any two styles or periods in design. However similar to Baroque style this facade may appear, the massive, unbroken pediment, decorated with cartouche and leafy garland, or the distinctive keystone-topped doorway with smaller unbroken pediment may be used. The latter is very practical. The use of a decorative doorway as the children enter the classroom makes a useful, evocative kernel design.

SMALL-GROUP RESEARCH PROJECTS

Some examples of small-group projects that relate to a study of England through its architecture include the following:

1.   Give children a set of slides or pictures of various buildings in England.   Have the children classify them according to various architectural styles.

2.   The various shades of color in the stained-glass windows are symbolic and have historical significance. Students could research the stained glass as well as some of the ecclesiastical symbols used in early cathedrals. They could make their own stained glass windows.

3.   Have children research famous British architects such as Sir Christopher Wren.

4.   Have children role-play being tourist guides.   They could take tourists through buildings like Westminster Abbey, St. Paul's Cathedral, the Tower of London, Buckingham Palace, Ockwell's Manor, or Windsor Castle.

5.   Have chidren role-play life in an English castle, palace, or manor.

6.   Have children research examples of English architecture in the United States.

7.   Students could estimate the sizes of spires, windows, or cathedrals, depth of arches, etc., and then verify them. They could actually mark the measurements on the cardboard representations of the kernel designs. (Each panel of the York Minster Cathedral looks about 6 inches in width, viewing it from one end of the cathedral; actually, each section is 3 feet long.)

8.   Have children make a time-line showing the different architectural styles in England. Historical events and famous people could be placed in the appropriate chronological order.

9.   Have students research the poets that are buried in Poet's Corner in Westminster Abbey, London. Their works could be read and shared with the class.

10. Students could correlate music with the various architectural periods.

11. Students could research the uses of the numerous rooms in Buckingham Palace, the roles of the people who are permitted to enter, the historical meaning of the changing of the Guards, the qualifications and ritual for becoming a member of the Queen's Guard, the numerous customs and traditions of England and the places where these customs occur.

12. Children could construct a model of a thatched cottage.

13. Children could research the advantages of the half-timber frame homes of the seventeenth century and the effective ways used to heat and light these homes. See if the students can discover why these homes are still standing after 300-500 years.

14. Since students seem to enjoy playing cards of any kind, pictures depicting windows, piers, or doorways of the six architectural periods could be glued on a deck of cards or tagboard pieces. Another set of cards could have the names of the six architectural periods. A third set of cards could have the names or pictures of historical buildings. The object would be to match the picture or the historical building with the appropriate architectural period. The game could follow the same rules as rummy, old maid, or solitaire.

SUMMARY

The architectural kernel designs create a historical setting for role-playing such experiences as a stroll through the open-air markets; travel down the medieval sidewalks and crooked stone streets; numerous tours of the magnificent historical buildings and walls that have withstood centuries of battles, internal struggle, and cultural changes; and, a walk on the same ground and in the same buldings that once bore the weight of barbaric tribes, Roman soldiers, Vikings, kings, queens, dukes, and merchants. Both the role-playing and research activities stimulated by the kernel designs should help students develop a better perspective of England's nineteen centuries of history. It should help them gain a better understanding and appreciation for the efforts of their ancestors.

REFERENCES

Fletcher, Sir Banister Flight. <u>A history of architecture on the comparative method</u>. New York: Scribner, 1963.

SUPPLEMENTARY BIBLIOGRAPHY

Amery, C. <u>Period houses and their details</u>. London: Architectural Press, 1974.

Banner, Robert. <u>Gothic architecture</u>. New York: Braziller, 1967.

Conant, K. J. <u>Carolingian and Romanesque architecture 800 to 1200.</u> Pelican History of Art Series, No. Z13. Baltimore: Penguin Press, 1965.

Hempel, E. <u>Baroque art and architecture in central Europe</u>. Pelican History of Art Series, No. Z22. Baltimore: Penguin Press, 1965.

Hindley, Geoffrey. <u>Great buildings of the world: Castles</u>. London: Hamlyn, 1968.

Lloyd, Seton, et al. <u>World architecture</u>. London: Hamlyn, 1966.

Nicholson, N. <u>Great houses of Britain</u>. New York: Spring Books, 1968.

Simson, O. G. <u>The Gothic cathedral</u>. New York: Pantheon, 1965.

Summerson, J. N. <u>Architecture in Britain, 1530 to 1830</u>. Baltimore: Penguin Press, 1953.

8 A Kernel Design of India

It is nearly impossible for the average American adult to comprehend the sprawling, shocking kaleidoscope of impossibilities that is India. While Indian engineers educated at Stanford or Michigan or Cornell prod ancient India into the twentieth century, Americans more often than not still think of India as nothing more than maharaji hunting tiger from elephant back, inscrutable Hindus, or scenes of religious bathing in the Ganges. The real, whole India is so elusive and so distinctively different from anything western that it may as well be just a magical word to a child.

It is important that children gain some appreciation for a culture so different from their own, if they are to truly understand their own culture. Through the kernel design concept, a child may be helped to discover differences without making value judgments, and to appreciate both the how and the why of the cultural disparities discovered between America and India. Through role-playing, discovery is made easier, and a few of the mysteries of India may be explored and compared.

NARRATIVE STATEMENT

India can be considered a country of extremes, more so than the United States. It is a country of limited affluence and extreme poverty. Even the poverty we see here in the United States is affluence compared to the poverty in India.

India is an overpopulated and underindustrialized country. Even for an agrarian society, India tends to be underproductive, and this, too, results in extremes. There· are extremes in family home life. Women remain subordinate to men and appear to enjoy it. There are extremes in religion. The strength of Hinduism is based on spirit and values, while Hatha yoga plays witness to the idea that the mind is all, to the exclusion of the body. This, too, can be considered an extreme. India is a country of seasonal extremes as well. One is easily reminded of this through simple research of illustrations portraying India in drought or India in monsoon. These seasonal extremes

76

contribute greatly to the pervading social extremes of wealth and poverty.

In spite of the fact that the basically Byzantine architecture of many of India's temples is not truly Indian, it does indeed typify one of the social extremes. Its use in the design of temples and royal tombs may be contrasted with views of crowded Indian streets where so many people are living and dying with no cover at all.

Technology in industry also represents extremes. The air-polluting, belching smokestacks and the large ships in the harbor stand in stark contrast to the cottage industries where entire families work on the manufacturing of a product. Cottage industries, likewise, are reflected in strong family orientation.

KERNELIZING IDEAS ABOUT INDIA

A quadrant approach is used to illustrate the extremes of India. The extreme of affluence can be recognized by the opulence of the Thakurji Temple in the Amber Province. Cut from a large piece of cardboard, the outlines of the Thakurji gateway and the typical pillars and statuary help to illustrate size and scope. Fig. 8-1 shows an illustration from which a kernel design could be made to symbolize affluence.

The Temple of Thakurji is only one of many possible selections to exemplify wealth, opulence, and the grand style as one of India's extremes. Unfortunately, while it is simple to locate, the typical photograph of such an ornate monument as an Indian temple will appear impossibly detailed. Reproduction in a realistic sense may seem difficult enough to deter you from its use. Don't be frightened by apparent complexities, but remember our request to simplify.

A creative kernel of Indian opulence need not, for example, be a naturalistic or photographically accurate reproduction of all, or any part of a temple, an item of costume, or even a traditional activity. Remember that a child's level of skill at drawing, or even visualizing, will effectively prevent photographic reproductions. It is more important, and this cannot be overemphasized, to create a _feeling_ of the time or place. This does not require exact duplication. We have elected to provide a line drawing in lieu of the original photograph to illustrate one level of simplification.

While superimposing minor detail from another building or temple on the generality of the Thakurji Temple might offend the purist, it will result in a very correct and effective kernel design. Clearly, if one small segment of the whole can be expected to evoke the impact of the whole, a capital or bit of sculpture from another, similar monument can be used as a guide to finish detail. The kernel concept is based upon the teacher's ability to create a feeling of time or place, and we should not be concerned with actuality or the degree of artistic license which can be allowed.

The architectural kernel of Indian opulence might, when finished, contain elements of many different buildings. It is what happens to the student during the inception of the kernel and after its completion that is important. If discovery occurs in the research and design process and within the social studies unit because of the kernel design, we will have satisfied the requirements of a creative classroom environment.

Fig. 8-1 The Thakurji (Vishnu) Temple (Jon Cobes)

A small corner of the room could be used to depict extreme poverty. An area, ideally with dirt floor, with no chairs, no table, no covering, can be sectioned off in the classroom. Within this area children can play the role of the crowded impoverished. If the idea of a dirt floor is repugnant, if your school maintenance staff is strongly opposed to such an idea, if the dirty clothes you may send home some days tend to make this a poor idea, use sand. Consider again our standby, the cardboard carton. A shallow carton, approximately four by eight feet, with a depth of six or so inches may be filled with an inch or more of playground sand to provide a very satisfactory illusion of the out-of-doors for many situations.

A third quadrant represents one extreme of the technology of India. The superstructure of ships in a harbor superimposed against smokestacks could be outlined and crafted as a two-dimensional cardboard cutout. This may be suspended from the ceiling. Fig. 8-2 depicts the simplicity of a kernel design to represent industry in India.

In contrast, quadrant four would represent the cottage industry concept where the entire family works on manufacturing a product by hand. Since the family group will often do its work outdoors in the sun, one could depict a very small courtyard adjacent to a small stucco dwelling. The arts of weaving and pottery are integrated into this quadrant. In the outdoor courtyard, much of the weaving of beautiful rugs and tapestries, as well as the dyeing and printing of materials takes place. The outdoors is also often used for eating (probably because of insufficient space and lighting in the dwelling). Fig. 8-3 depicts one of many ways in which a kernel design might evoke an image of cottage industry in India. The line drawing illustrates a composite kernel design, usable for a cottage industry area or for an illustration of Indian poverty. More important, this kernel design illustrates the degree to which simplicity can be effective in developing a creative classroom environment. A live branch suspended so as to appear to grow from the wall, will create a feeling of "place" for most children. When this simple device is accompanied by all the other child-produced trappings of that place, you will have produced a kernel design that will evoke a role-related response from the class.

A marketplace is set up in the center of this quasi-city, in which children role-play the castes of India and experience the processes of haggling, barter, and purchase. Setting up a marketplace should be as simple as the kernels already produced. Remember that no special provision need be made for space, furnishings, or atmosphere. Most of what is needed is already prepared. The kernelized quadrants encourage completion of the unit and provide an illusion of place to stimulate further activity. Child-researched and child-produced properties, such as typical items of apparel, will enhance the marketplace atmosphere. While your market is no more than your class desks, role-playing will make any item donated for use a "real" piece of Indian goods.

The results of technology, both modern and ancient, can be seen side-by-side at the marketplace. Tradeable items such as simple domestic housewares, kitchenware, or homemade pottery are "sold" at the market-place. By actually dividing the class into four groups corresponding to the kernel design quadrant and giving them some sort of legal tender in keeping

Fig. 8-2 Modern Manufacturing (Jon Cobes)

with their status in the community, a strong object lesson on affluence and poverty may be experienced. The affluent and industrial folk would be given money; the family group would be given practically no money; and the impoverished would be given nothing. To illustrate the caste system, the impoverished would not be permitted to mingle with the other people.

In order to kernelize the people of India in action, one should also focus on the details of costume and unique properties such as the sari, the turban, the scarf, the marketplace and the kinds of things that are in it that say "India."

Fig. 8-3   A Kernel Design of Cottage Industry   (James Thorpe)

SMALL-GROUP ACTIVITIES

Examples of small-group activities related to India include the following:

1.   Have children collect different spices and herbs used in Indian cooking. Have them discover why a number of people are vegetarians.

2.   Have children follow recipes and prepare Indian dishes using primitive means of cooking.

3.   Have children prepare appropriate background music.

4.   Burn incense in a safe place. Have the children research the use of incense.

5.   Have children look in catalogs and find exports and imports of India.   They could set up a store for selling items such as cards, trinkets, or posters of India, or they could incorporate the sales into the haggling experiences at the marketplace.

6.   Have children become pen pals with children from India.

7.   Since a large group of people in India are farmers, one group of children could be responsible for planting a crop or small garden outside the school.   The children wouldn't be digging with very sophisticated tools and machinery. This will make them realize that the farmer's life is not easy, especially without modern irrigation. Children would not be allowed to water the garden. If the ground is ruined by either too much or too little rain, this will lead them to understand how people depend on each other, not only in the village or city or country, but in the world. This would lead to a greater understanding of how people manage under varying geographical conditions of climate and terrain to meet their needs, to utilize their natural recources, and to relate to each other economically and socially.

SUMMARY

As children interact within the proposed kernel designs, India will come alive.   They will learn that there are a vast number of languages, dresses, traditions, superstitions, and religions in India. They will experience the real meaning of the caste system.   They will realize that there are no special homes for older people, because, in the family system, everyone is always cared for, not only parents, but uncles, aunts, and counsins.   There are no special teen-age clubs because there is no dating system as such.   Many marriages are still arranged by parents or other close relatives.

The small-group activities will bring to life a microcosm of India. In fact, these role-centered activities are the core of the integrated unit. They help children identify themselves with the real-life emotional experiences of the people of India about whom they're reading and studying.   The emotional experience itself will be remembered far longer than the mere researched facts.

9 A Kernel Design Related to the American Melting-Pot Cuisines

The kernel design technique spans all grade levels, subject areas, and disciplines. This chapter exemplifies its use for either middle-school children or junior-high school students. In contrast to major emphasis on stage-craft representations, this chapter focuses on a higher level of research in which students discover specific details regarding why people eat what they do, when and how they eat, and what people should eat as a nutritional diet. Although the major focus is home economics, this emphasis is not restrictive. As demonstrated in the British primary schools, cooking and baking can form an important part of every child's experiential learning. Furthermore, nutrition education, a goal that can be achieved naturally through this unit, should become an integral part of the curriculum at all grade levels. Wise selection of food is basic. The kernel design approach to nutrition can make this topic come alive, not only in the classroom but in the daily lives of the students.

NARRATIVE STATEMENT

As each group of immigrants arrived in America, so did their Old World customs, traditions, arts, crafts, and food. Today these traditions have been shared and lines of distinction have blurred. Among the things that the immigrants found easy to share across language barriers were their culinary skills. Many of these skills have survived and are to be found in ethnic restaurants across the country. The cuisines of Spain, China, Italy, and France have been selected arbitrarily as examples for this chapter.

Spanish cuisine

Spain, like America, is a mélange of many cultures. Spain, meaning "Hidden Land" because of its high mountains, was first discovered by the Moorish Arabs who remained in southern Spain for over 800 years. The flamenco dance and the national sport of bullfighting were inherited from the Moors. The Moors planted the vineyards and olive trees from which today's sherry and olive oil are exported around the world. The Romans were next to invade, arriving about 205 B.C., and remaining the dominant culture for over 300 years. There is little evidence, however, of Roman influence, except as reflected in the language. The cuisine of Spain bears little resemblance to that of Italy except in the use of some of the same basic ingredients.

Moorish influence is reflected in the use of Oriental spices such as cinnamon, cumin, saffron, and cloves. Fruits cooked in meat and rice dishes, almonds, and sugarcane were introduced by the Moors. Pasta is rarely seen in Spanish cooking, and Spanish food is not hot, in the spicy sense of the word. From Mexico and Peru, Spain inherited a taste for the tomato, sweet pepper (pimento), chocolate, and vanilla. These foods and spices were probably brought back from the voyages of Columbus.

Generally speaking, Spanish cooking is based on the use of rice and olive oil. Other characteristics are the use of parsley, a delicate flavor of orange in meat and poultry dishes, use of pimento and paprika (a spice ground from pimentos), and use of garlic, onions, and tomatoes. The Spanish still rely upon fresh foods because of lack of adequate storage and refrigeration. In the marketplace, you will find everything displayed creatively, with fresh food trucked in each day.

The Spanish begin their day early with a light breakfast. Lunch is the main meal and is served around 2:00 p.m. Supper is eaten at 10:00 p.m. or later. There is a great deal of snacking on tapas between meals. Tapas are bite-size nibbles which may be eaten any hour of the day.

A formal Spanish meal begins with sherry, which prepares the palate for the meal. Gaspacho is a typical Spanish soup made from tomatoes, garlic, olive oil, vinegar, and various vegetables and is served cold. The Spanish are also famous for seafood recipes. Vegetables are sometimes served as a solo first course or in casseroles or stew; dessert is usually fruit. Sweets are accompanied by coffee, tea, or chocolate between 6:00 and 7:00 p.m. as a before-dinner snack. Few Spanish kitchens have an oven. The Spanish use a grill for fast cooking and do not regularly bake.

Chinese cuisine

Chinese cuisine has become quite popular in the United States in the past few years. The method employed in preparing a dish is almost ritual. Infinite care is given to each ingredient, and the Chinese cook is totally absorbed in the artistic creation. Confucius ordained that there should be the use of vegetables in the ratio of two-thirds vegetables to one-third meat. Meat is used, therefore, to add flavor and enhance but not to overpower the dish.

To the Chinese, the cutting of the ingredient is a real art. Meat is sliced thinly and against the grain. Crisp vegetables are cut diagonally into thin, even slices. Mushrooms or scallions are cut straight. The preparation time spent in cutting the food is much greater than the actual cooking. The Chinese use a choy dak (cleaver) for cutting, slicing, and grating. After each ingredient is prepared, it is put in a separate pile or dish until all the ingredients are assembled. The Chinese use a wok to stir-fry, steam, and deep-fry, or as a saucepan and stew kettle. The wok is a wide-mouthed, shallow, metallic bowl with handles on both sides. Food is cooked quickly (to conserve fuel) until each ingredient is just done. Each dish in a Chinese meal is a contrast in taste and texture. Considerable emphasis is placed on serving attractively and garnishing.

Only one-sixth of the land in China is fertile, and the Chinese cook must be highly skilled and inventive, as every available ingredient is used. Leftovers are very seldom thrown away; they are either dried or pickled for later use. Beef is not commonly used because of the lack of grazing land. Dairy products are seldom used.

Ingredients which dominate Chinese cuisine include soy sauce, monosodium glutamate (which enhances, like salt, the flavor of many foods), peanut oil, rice, noodles, garlic, wine, bamboo shoots, dried fish, mushrooms, fresh ginger root, water chestnuts, lotus root, and bean curd. Three other ingredients Americans talk about because of their uniqueness (but which are not used often because of their cost) are shark's fin, 100-year-old eggs, and bird's nests. The shark's fins are used in soups for their interesting flavor and thickening effect. Bird nests are used in soups for their gelatinous quality. Normally, no bread, butter, or milk is served with a Chinese meal.

It is easy to identify the unique utensils the Chinese use in eating. The chopsticks can be quite difficult to master. The formal Chinese meal usually consists of soup and main dishes which are brought to the table at the same time. Each guest has a pair of chopsticks, a porcelain spoon, a rice bowl, a small dish for dipping condiments, and a soup dish. They share the food from common serving bowls on the table. Tea is usually served at the end of the meal.

Italian cuisine

Italian food is often called the "mother cuisine." It is the source of western cuisine, and was the first fully developed cuisine in Europe. Italy taught France, in 1532, the art of making pastry, desserts, cakes, cream puffs, and ices. The Italian cuisine began simply. Pula, the staple dish of the Romans, is a mush made from millet or spelt grain. The Romans cultivated vegetables and fruits, such as cabbages and apples; as they began to conquer other nations, they imported different foods such as apricots from Armenia, melons and peaches from Persia, and dates from Africa. The "central market" concept is of Roman origin and evolved from their affection for a wide variety of foods. They were very fond of meat. They used no sugar, but they did use honey. The Romans are credited with the invention of the omelet, cheesecake, and as many as 13 varieties of cheese. With the invasion of the barbarians, in the third century A.D., the recipes the Romans had were kept by the monasteries. The Islamic invasions affected southern Italy in the ninth century, when ice cream and sherbet desserts and various sweets, such as cane sugar, were introduced. In the eleventh century, the Crusaders finally plated sugar and also buckwheat. In the twelfth century, the Italian economy became stable for the first time in centuries, and spices were brought back again. Meals began to have three or four courses. The art of building up pyramids of food on serving platters and the custom of surprising guests with ingeniously disguised foods, such as a roast of meat which turned out to be fish, was begun.

In the thirteenth century, a cookbook was printed which contained a recipe for pasta and, in 1475, Platina authored a cookbook which was widely accepted and contained classical cooking recipes. In the sixteenth century, the first modern cooking academy was established in Florence. As the Italian Renaissance progressed, cooking became more varied, but pasta remained the mainstay of the meal. When Catherine de Medici traveled to France to marry, she took along her entourage of cooks who introduced great cooking in France.

Basic ingredients found in Italian dishes include over 40 different kinds of pasta, cheeses, sausage, salami, fish, asparagus, spinach, tomato, fresh or dried bundles of parsley, sweet basil, wild marjoram, thyme, rosemary, sage, tarragon, bay leaves, oregano, mint, myrtle, fennel seeds, juniper berries, cloves, coriander, saffron, celery, onions, shallots, garlic, lemon juice, vinegar, and olives. With all these flavors to choose from, there are many different dishes. The midday meal is the principal meal of the day and is eaten at home. It is rather simple, beginning with pasta or soup followed by a main dish of fish or meat, vegetable or greens, cheese or fruit or both. Elaborate desserts are served when guests are present, and rich, dark espresso coffee is a tradition.

French cuisine

France was once divided into 30 provinces. While these provinces no longer exist, they each still retain vestiges of autonomy in their own ways of preparing special dishes. The French still rely on fresh foods as do the Spanish. In most villages in France, there is at least one general store where farmers leave whatever is ready to sell that day. The supply varies but the produce is always fresh. There are bakeries wherever there is a community, and all bakeries sell the irregularly shaped loaves of light and dark bread along with the pastries and other baked goods unique to each region. Northern France is basically Germanic in cultural origin, and the south is Latin. Cheese comes from the highland meadows, and oysters are harvested along the northern and western coasts. The major produce of each region varies greatly because of differences in terrain and climate.

There are two cuisines in France today: the provincial cooking and haute cuisine, or gourmet classic cooking. A typical provincial dinner will vary according to the habits of the region and the season. Dinner is usually served in the middle of the day, at home if possible. It is a basically simple meal unless it is for a special occasion such as "the first frost," or "the last strawberry tart until next year." France has been slightly Americanized in that some lunch breaks have been shortened from the traditional two hours to forty-five minutes. However, in the provinces, the main meal is still a leisurely experience. Conversation at a French meal is almost as essential to the art of eating as the food itself.

Hors d'oeuvre is the first course of the French meal. It may be plain or elaborate, hot or cold, and is designed to tease the palate. The main dish may be fish, meat, or fowl. If no vegetables are in the dish, sometimes a vegetable will accompany it. After this, a plain salad of green lettuce is served with a simple vinegar-and-oil dressing. Desserts are seldom served except on Sundays or other feast days. Cheeses may be served instead, after which come ripe fruits such as cherries, plums, currants or figs, and coffee.

Classic French cooking includes subtle sauces, soufflés, truffles or gloriously decorated dishes. Much of the cooking is done in earthenware pots, copper and enamel pans. Care is taken in the planning of the menu. This cuisine is demanding and precise. There are many recipes that can be prepared for each dish. Chefs must train for many years to be able to prepare each dish to perfection. Sparkling crystal, gleaming silver, and immaculate linens are requisites in classic French service.

RESEARCHING ILLUSTRATIONS AND RESOURCES

Although this unit focuses on the cuisines of Spain, Italy, France, and China, any kernel design plan that evokes an image of these four countries can be used. Accordingly, in addition to the food itself, menus, language, customs, national sports, unique architecture, renowned monuments, or costumes could be used. The major criteria to consider are whether the kernel designs create an atmosphere associated with each country that motivates students to research the native cuisines in relation to and beyond the kernel designs. Valuable resource materials for this unit are available through the National Dairy Council which is a nonprofit research and educational organization of the dairy industry. Its purpose is to contribute to the achievement of optimal health by providing leadership in nutrition research and nutrition education based on the concept of a balanced diet in accordance with scientific recommendations. In January 1970, the Dairy Council was officially designated an educational/scientific institution by the U.S. Department of the Treasury, Internal Revenue Service. Nutrition education materials can be obtained from the National Dairy Council office. The materials are designed and developed to meet the varied needs of professional, educational, and consumer groups and to provide authentic information and teaching aids about dairy foods and their contributions to nutritional well-being.

KERNELIZING THE AMERICAN MELTING-POT CUISINES
AND SMALL-GROUP ACTIVITIES

The kernel design technique may take several finished forms. Architectural detail is not the "sine qua non" of this creative concept. We have repeatedly emphasized role-playing or creative dramatics as basic to the creative classroom experience. This sample unit is included because the kernel design is, in fact, one of action and interaction rather than one of solely scenic elements.

If you have visited Europe, or if you dream a bit by looking at typical travel brochures, you may have noticed that restaurants around the world often look quite alike. Red-checked tablecloths and candles in old Chianti bottles do not make a French or Italian café. To kernelize by simply "setting the stage" with red-checked tablecloths and candles for a study area such as this would not at all assure success. Kernelize action, not places. What makes a French sidewalk café different from its Italian or Spanish counterpart is the people. Language and cuisine are easily observed aspects of a culture and, while hardly exhaustive, they are often more unique than architecture or dress.

Spain

Vineyards, olive trees, high mountains, a bullfight scene, and a flamenco dancer are but a few ideas of what might be used to imply a Spanish decor for a kernel design of Spain. If the class is divided into four groups, have one group research the following areas:

1. Find out the characteristics of Spanish cuisine. What makes it unique? What ingredients are used? How did it get started? When do the Spaniards eat their meals? What are some common dishes?

2. Describe tapas. When are they eaten?

3. Study olive oil. Why is it used so extensively in Spanish cooking? What are its good characteristics? Its bad characteristics?

4. "Discover" what paella is and how it is used in Spanish cuisine. How is it prepared and why is it done this way? Why does Spain use one predominant method of cookery?

5. Compare the differences between Spanish cooking and Mexican cooking.

6. After the students research and discover answers to the above questions and statements, they could pick one dish typical of Spanish cuisine and prepare it for the class to enjoy as they share their new knowledge about Spanish cuisine with the entire class.

China

The kernel design for Chinese cuisine could focus on the unique preparations -separate bowls for each ingredient, the cleaver, the wok, and chopsticks. Distinctive Chinese characters could be used to designate the various foods.

Examples of small-group activities could include the following:

1. Find out the characteristics of Chinese cuisine. What makes it unique? What ingredients are used? When do the Chinese eat their

meals? How are meals served?

2.   Describe the cooking equipment, namely the wok. How is it used?

3.   How are the ingredients used in dishes prepared? Find out everything you can about a cleaver.

4.   Learn how to use chopsticks and be able to demonstrate to the class.

5.   Compare Chinese cooking as written and described in cookbooks with cooking in a modern-day Chinese restaurant.

6.   After the students research and discover Chinese cuisine, they too could select one typical dish and prepare it for the class to taste as they share their new knowledge about the cuisine of China.

France

A very natural kernel design for French cuisine is the streetside café. To distinguish it from other cafés, French signs could be posted; also, the Eiffel Tower could be shown in the background. Silver, china, and linens (or some reasonable facsimile) could adorn the tables. Menus would be in French.
Examples of small-group activities could include the following:

1.   What are the two cuisines of France? Describe their differences and similarities.

2.   Pick one region of France and discover the foods unique to that area. Compare it with a different region.

3.   Describe a typical French dinner. How does it differ from a typical American meal?

4.   What are the basic sauces used in different French dishes? How are they used? Are they similar to any typical American sauces?

5.   What is a soufflé? Prepare one. What new cooking techniques did you learn?

After the above activities have been completed, the students will decide on a provincial French dish or a classical dish and prepare it for the class. They will also present their discoveries to the class.

Italy

The kernel design depicting Italy could include a representation of the Leaning Tower of Pisa and pasta hanging to dry. Research activities could include the following:

1.   Find out the characteristics of Italian food. What are the unique qualities? What are some common ingredients? Of what does a

typical meal consist? How do the regions of Italy differ?

2.   What is pasta? Find out how it is made. How many varieties are there? What are their differences?

3.   Read about Italy's cheeses. What did you discover?

4.   Ice cream and sherbet are popular desserts that are served in most Italian restaurants. Is this true of all Italy?

5.   Compare Italian cooking as you discovered it with that of a local Italian restaurant.

Some general activities could include the following:

1.   After discussing the typical spices used by the four countries, students could be blindfolded and asked to guess which country's sample food they were tasting.

2.   Have students research and locate the names of famous restaurants.

3.   Have students discuss how these four foreign cuisines have influenced American cooking.

4.   Have students list the visible signs of foreign cuisine seen in our typically modern food to show that our country is the "melting pot of the world."

5.   Have students research how foreign cooks measure food quantities in metric terms. Using this information and foreign cookbooks, the students could convert several basic recipes from metric measurements into customary units or they could convert one of their favorite recipes into metrics.

As stated in Chapter 4, one unit can often serve as an introduction to another unit. This unit could lead naturally into an informative, authentic study of nutrition. According to Kelly (1977), few contemporary concerns approach the gravity of nutrition education. "This subject is not limited to a single geographical location; age group, racial, ethnic, or religious classification; educational level, socio-economic class; or nation, whether developed, underdeveloped, or developing. This pervasive concern involves 'what we need to know' in contrast to 'what is nice to know' " (p.2).

The study of nutrition need not be passive. Students can be involved in activities such as the following:

1.   Have students act the role of tourists in Spain, France, Italy, and China. They would order foods that reflect a balanced diet using foods that are unique to each of these countries.

2.   Begin with a list of pictures of varied international foods and chart a balanced daily diet for a week.

3.   Have   the   students   categorize   food   according   to   four

classificatons: foods that are nutritional and orally safe for dental hygiene; foods that are nutritional but not orally safe; foods that are nonnutritional but orally safe; and foods that are nonnutritional and orally hazardous.   The use of a flannelgraph board would work well for this activity.

These are only samples of activities that can be used to make nutrition an interesting study.   Other activities related to nutrition are suggested in the materials from the Dairy Council, to which reference was made earlier in this chapter.

SUMMARY

The different foods brought to America from other countries testify that America is truly the melting pot of the world. A kernel design approach to the study of several cuisines, exemplified in this chapter by Spanish, French, Italian, and Chinese cooking, should lead to a greater understanding and appreciation of various ethnic groups and their contributions to one of America's favorite pastimes - eating. Furthermore, this unit leads naturally into a study of nutritional education - a topic that should be of vital concern to everyone.

* * *

Free information on nutrition
can be obtained from:

National Dairy Council
6300 North River Road
Rosemont, Illinois 60018

REFERENCES

Kelly, J.   National Dairy Council's nutrition education materials, 1977.
Rosemont, Ill.: National Dairy Council Publications, 1977.

SUPPLEMENTARY BIBLIOGRAPHY

American Dietetic Association.   Food facts talk back.   Chicago, Ill.:
American Dietetic Association, 1974.

Carey, R.L.; Vyhmeister, I. B.; and Hudson, J. S. Common sense nutrition, a
guide to good health for your family. Mountain View, Cal.: Pacific Press,
1971.

Deutsch, R. M. The family guide to better food and better health. Des
Moines, Iowa: Meredith, 1971.

Guthrie, H. A. Introductory nutrition, 2nd ed. St. Louis, Mo.: Mosby, 1971.

Lappe, Frances M. Diet for a small planet. New York: Ballantine, 1971.

Levine, M. I., and Seligmann, J. H.   Your overweight child.   New York:
World, 1970.

Mayer, Jean. Overweight--causes, cost, and control. Englewood Cliffs, N.J.:
Prentice-Hall, 1968.

Sebrell, W.H., and Haggerty, J. J. Food and nutrition. New York: Time-Life
Books, 1967.

Stare, F. J. Eating for good health. New York: Simon & Schuster, 1969.

Stuart, R. B., and Davis, B. Slim chance in a fat world. Champaign, Ill.:
Research Press, 1972.

U.S. Dept. of Agriculture. Food for us all, yearbook of agriculture.
Washington: Government Printing Office, 1969.

White, P. L. Let's talk about food. Acton, Me.: Publishing Sciences Group,
1974.

10 A Kernel Design Applied to a Science Unit on Six Simple Machines

The kernel design process can support the development of most elementary scientific concepts. If a goal of teachers of science is to lead students to an intuitive realization that science exists all around us and influences many aspects of daily life, then the kernel design, which provides motivation for children to become miniature researchers within a creatively designed environment, can be an invaluable tool. . For illustrative purposes, this chapter shows how the kernel design can be used in teaching a unit on six simple machines. Above all, it shows how the kernel design unifies rather than divides science and social studies.

NARRATIVE STATEMENT

The history of the early development of simple machines is testimony to the survival instinct in man. All of the simple machines evolved as solutions to problems that man encountered in coping with his environment. When early man used a stone knife to split the skin of an animal, he used a primitive wedge; when he moved a boulder in front of the opening of his cave with the aid of a strong branch, he was using the simple machine called the lever. We can assume that early man also noticed that a round object moves more easily than one that is not round, and the first wheel may have been a row of logs to roll loads for short distances. When King Nebuchadnezzar built the beautifully terraced Hanging Gardens of Babylon for his mountain princess, he irrigated them by means of a series of huge, turning screws which lifted water up to the gardens from the Euphrates River. The Egyptians could never have built the massive and magnificent pyramids had they not been aware of the principles of the inclined plane, the wheel, and the pulley. No one person can be credited with the invention of any of the simple machines. All must have evolved out of need and generations of observations of solutions to the vexing problems of a hostile environment. Early man certainly did not know that he was using simple machines. He must only have known that these tools enabled him to accomplish certain tasks with less effort. It was left to

Egyptian and Greek scholars to document scientific reasons for the efficiency of the simple machines.

As man discovered new uses for simple machines, he was able to move from primitive to more civilized ways of living, and the history of civilization almost parallels the everwidening and everwiser (in most cases) use of machines. But no matter how complex today's machines appear, they are really combinations of six simple machines - the lever, the inclined plane, the wedge, the screw, the wheel and axle, and the pulley. It is these six simple machines which man, through the ages, has learned to use in a great variety of ways to do his work more easily. Today, almost every activity in daily life depends in some way on machines.

Simple machines appear so commonly in modern life that many are not recognized by children as machines at all - the stairway, for instance, or the nail or the fishing pole. Other simple machines operate with such ease that no thought is given to the difficulty of the task without their aid - the pulley on the flagpole, for instance. A study of simple machines must emphasize recognition and appreciation of the usefulness of simple machines.

RESEARCHING ILLUSTRATIONS

Scientific illustrations of simple machines can be found in encyclopedias and science and other technical reference books. Illustrations of simple machines in everyday use can easily be found in most general reading material. Brochures, magazines, mail order catalogs, and newspapers, would be good places to look. That unique element which says "simple machine" would perhaps not be any one illustration or any single machine. That element would have to be found in the diversity of examples of simple machines, inferring their widespread existence. The lasting impression should be the awareness that we are literally surrounded by simple, basic machines.

KERNELIZING IDEAS AND RELATED ACTIVITIES

In the initial learning stage of the kernel design, the children should become familiar with the vocabulary related to simple machines and learn to recognize the six simple machines. All terms should either be explained or demonstrated. It should never be assumed that elementary school children have a command of technical language. A basic list of words which elementary school children should understand while studying simple machines could include: compound machine, effort, energy, force, friction, fulcrum, gravity, inclined plane, inertia, lever, machine, machine age, mechanical advantage, pulley, resistance, screw, simple machine, wedge, wheel and axle, and work. Vocabulary words can be taught in the following ways:

1.   Children could print the important terms and their meanings on large sheets of poster paper. Display these posters on the walls of the classroom where they are visible to all children for reference. Additional terms and their meanings should be added as needed.

2.   Have children keep a "word bank" of all new terms related to the six basic machines.

3.   Use these terms in spelling and language arts during the time period of the study.

4.   Encourage children to use these terms in their language as they give reports and demonstrations.

5.   Record a cassette tape of definitions of terms.   Include in a packet with the tape, illustrations, diagrams, and other aids to which children can refer while listening to the tape.

6.   Many of these terms can be explained best through experiments. For example:

work can be explained by having a child push against the wall of the classroom. He should push very hard until he is tired. Then another child goes to the chalk board and picks up an eraser. The question: Which child did the most work? The answer: Only the child who picked up the eraser worked, because, scientifically, work is not done until an object is moved from one place to another.

friction can be explained by having the children first try to slide in a stony section of the playground and then try to slide on ice or a waxed surface. The question: On which surface could you slide more easily? The explanation: The stones caused resistance, or friction, making sliding difficult.

gravity can be demonstrated by having children drop objects. The question: Why do the objects fall down and not up or sideways? The answer: Gravity is the attraction which pulls all objects toward the center of the earth.

compound machine could be demonstrated by displaying for the class common tools which are combinations of two or more simple machines, for instance, a meat grinder, which is a combination of wheel and axle, screw and wedge. Another example would be a pair of scissors, which combines a double lever with a wedge on each tip.

To learn to recognize the six simple machines, assign an equal number of children to research and demonstrate each simple machine. In a class of 24 children, for instance, six groups of four children could be selected. Each group would be responsible for researching the same simple machine throughout the study.

To prepare the kernel design for recognition, each group might assemble a sign labeling the simple machine being demonstrated, a large cardboard model or drawing of the machine (which would be very simple, making clear the basic design and purpose of the machine) and a poster showing colorful, illustrative examples of the machine. Each group would arrange its display in a different part of the room. The signs labeling the simple machines could be suspended from the ceiling. It would be the goal of each group to teach recognition of that group's simple machine and the principles of its operation, list for the class as many commonly used examples of that simple machine as possible and to explain how and why that simple machine makes work easier. The cardboard model would help to teach recognition. The poster would be a visual aid in listing examples. Some groups might want to include posters describing the efficiency and mechanical advantage factors of their machines. Following the presentations, all kernel design models, sign labels and posters would be displayed in the classroom for the remainder of the study.

To help children discover that simple machines exist everywhere and anywhere, each group would be assigned to search the school and schoolyard for an example of its machine which is in daily use within the school situation. The children would be cautioned to keep their examples secret, thereby heightening the excitement of the project. Each group would then lead the class to its example, explaining why that machine was selected. In each case, the simple machine selected should be in common daily use and the children should be able to explain how it works, why it is useful, and why we are dependent upon it. Following are examples of simple machines which might be selected in a school situation:

Inclined plane

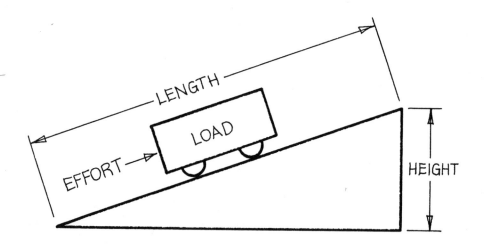

Fig. 10-1 Inclined Plane is Essentially a Surface Raised at One End
(James Thorpe)

The group working with the inclined plane could lead the class to the stairway. Ask the class to imagine that the stairway has disappeared. Question: How would you get up and down? The class would realize that without the stairway access from floor to floor would be difficult. A rope or ladder might be suggested as a crude solution to the problem of access. These would permit access from floor to floor, but in an inefficient manner. It is possible that an improvement to the stairway might be suggested. By adding rollers and electricity to the inclined plane of the stairway, a conveyor belt or escalator could be developed, thereby reducing the effort needed to climb the stairway.

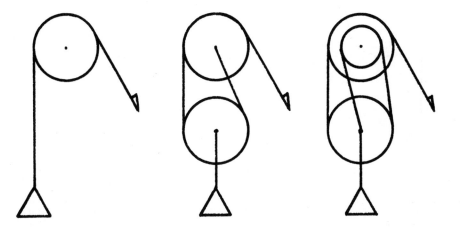

Fig. 10-2 Pulley (James Thorpe)

The group working with the pulley could lead the children to the flagpole, arranging beforehand to have the flag down. Ask the class to imagine that the rope and pulley have disappeared. Question: How do you get the flag up the pole? Possible answers might include shinnying up the pole with the flag or leaning a ladder (inclined plane) against the flagpole. The class will soon realize that without the pulley on the flagpole, no simple or safe method remains for hoisting the flag to the top of the pole. This would be a good opportunity to demonstrate that one major advantage of the pulley rests in its ability to reverse the direction of movement.

Another advantage of the pulley is its ability to increase "mechanical advantage." After experimenting with the lever, come back to the pulley as a lifting device. Show that, like some other simple machines, the pulley may be used in multiples of itself to result in an arithmetically predictable increase in lifting power. For example:

1. effort = 50 lbs.   2. effort = 50 lbs.   3. effort = 50 lbs.

    work = 50 lbs.   work = 100 lbs.   work = 150 lbs.

    advantage = 1:1   advantage = 2:1   advantage = 3:1

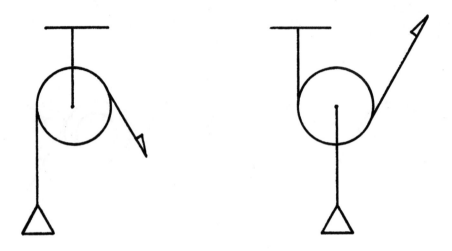

Fig. 10-3 Fixed and Moveable Pulleys. A fixed pulley is first-class lever, while a moveable pulley is second-class lever.   (James Thorpe)

Children can discover that this mechanical advantage is the same as that which accrues to the lever or the lever and fulcrum, and can be calculated in much the same manner.

Wheel and axle

The group working with the wheel and axle could lead the class to a school bus (compound machine). Ask the class to imagine that the wheels and axles have disappeared. Possibly, it could be suggested that the wheels and axles from all of vehicles have disappeared. Question: Will the school bus be able to move along the road? If not, why not? The answer should involve friction. The class should soon realize that there is no substitute for the wheel and axle. At this time, if it has not already been mentioned, it could be pointed out that the wheel is considered one of the most valuable inventions of all time. The class could be asked to suggest alternate methods of moving the bus along the road; however, no other method can adequately replace the wheel.

Wheel and axle, which acts as a first-class lever, is two wheels joined together and turning on a common axle.

Gear wheels, like the principle of the wheel and axle, they can act as multipliers of either force or speed.

Fig. 10-4 Wheel and Axle (James Thorpe)

Wedge

The group working with the wedge could lead the class to the school cafeteria. A member of the group could take a knife and peel or slice a potato or carrot. Have on hand unsliced and unpeeled carrots or potatoes. Ask the class to imagine that there is no such machine as a knife. Question: How would the cooks slice or peel the carrots or potatoes? Suggestions from the class might include various types of cutting tools; the group would point out that all cutting tools are wedges.   The class should realize that all operations such as cutting, slicing, peeling, and splitting are dependent on the use of the wedge. An alternate activity for the wedge would be to have a girl sewing two pieces of cloth together. Imagine that the needle does not exist. Question: How could she join the cloth together? The children would soon realize that all piercing instruments are wedges and that sewing as it is known today would be impossible without the simple machine called the wedge.

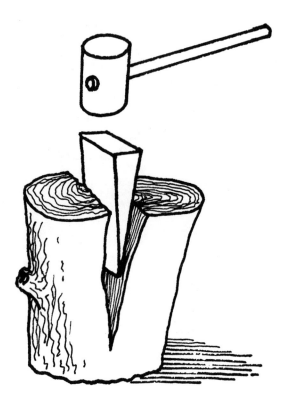

Fig. 10-5 Wedge: Two Inclined Planes (James Thorpe)

Lever

The group working with the lever could lead the class to a place where scissors are kept. Explanation should be made that scissors are considered to be a double lever. A member of the group would cut out an intricate design with the scissors, while requesting that another member of the class produce the same design without the use of the scissors. Question: If scissors did not exist, how would cutting operations be handled? Class members might suggest knives or razor blades as substitutes for scissors. It should be pointed out that they would be awkward substitutes for scissors. An alternative demonstration could involve the use of the stapler.

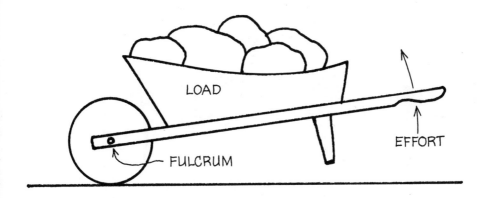

a. First-class Lever: The fulcrum may be at any point between the effort
   and the load.   (James Thorpe)

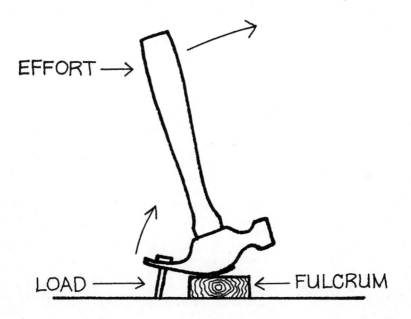

b. Second-class Lever: The load may be anywhere between the fulcrum and
   the effort.   (James Thorpe)

Fig. 10-6   Levers

FULCRUM →

EFFORT →

LOAD

c. Third-class Lever: The effort may be applied anywhere between the
   fulcrum and the load.   (James Thorpe)

Another interesting example of the lever may be explained in the classroom
using a bathroom scale and a small plank or board up to six feet in length and
strong enough to hold the weight of one child. Weigh the plank by centering
it on the scale. Then weigh the plank with one end on the floor and one end
on the scale. What is the difference (the ratio) and why? Weigh a child on
the scale. Weigh the same child while standing at the middle of the plank,
one end on the floor and one end on the scale. Weigh the child as he moves in
either direction, toward the floor or toward the scale. Discover the pattern
of change and the reason why. Have a child try to lift another child without
mechanical aid. Have the child lift the same person by means of the lever.
What is the difference? Can we predict the amount of effort required to
move (lift) a certain weight? How can this be done using our simple
experimental system?

Screw

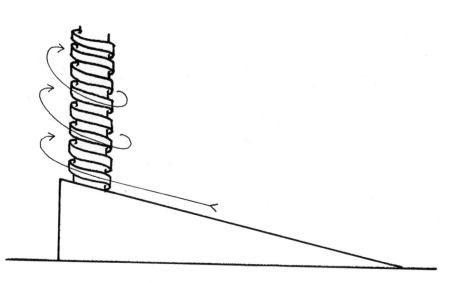

Fig. 10-7   Screw is essentially an inclined plane wrapped around a cylinder
to form a helical thread.   (James Thorpe)

The group working with the screw could lead the class to the school shop or
manual training area where members of the group would secure a board in a
vise. Ask the class to imagine there is no such thing as a screw. Question:
How can the board be secured? A child might suggest nailing the board, but
the group should point out that the nail is a wedge (another simple machine)
and that a vise is intended for the temporary securing of objects. Also, the
group could demonstrate how a vise can secure an object and then release it
without damaging the object.

Returning to the classroom, it could be pointed out that the doorknob on
the classroom door represents a wheel and axle, screws hold the door hinges
in place, nails hold the door molding in place, pencils represent a type of
lever, etc. The children should by now be able to recognize many simple
machines and should have developed an awareness and appreciation for their
usefulness in everyday life.

Fig. 10-8 represents the historical development of simple machines as
seen through the "eye of history."

Fig. 10-8   The Kernel Design in Historical Development.   The sketch shows a continuous mural depicting the evolution of simple machines and the comparative chronology.   Children can do most of this mural by researching dates, and using cutouts from magazines to illustrate development through man's history.   Many   more details can be shown, of course, than can be included in this small illustration.

(James Thorpe)

The time line, each line segment representing 1,000 years, would be suspended from the ceiling with the "eye of history" placed beneath it.   The time line represents the long span of time during which simple machines have been used and the eye represents flashbacks into the past.

The purposes of this kernel design of history would be three-fold: to help children to envision a time in history when crude simple machines were the only machines available; to demonstrate to children that the progress of civilization parallels the development of machines; and to introduce the concept of the machine age.

All six simple machines were devised and used by primitive peoples to fulfill needs long before man had developed the scientific knowledge to explain the efficiency of these machines.   Each group of children would research and enact an early use of its simple machine.   These enactments could be in the form of scenes or vignettes, or they could be in the form of poster drawings. In all cases the children should be prepared to explain why the simple machine being demonstrated was indispensable in the situation being enacted. Each group would mark on the time line the approximate date of its scene. Following are suggestions for prehistorical and historical scenes:

1.   Wedge - Children could enact a scene showing a primitive man skinning and cutting up an animal with a wedgelike stone tool or celt, or the primitive man could be throwing a spear, the spearhead being the wedge. Question: Could primitive man have hunted and prepared meat and skins without these wedgelike tools.   Discussion should convince children that without these tools primitive man could not have survived.

2.   Lever - Children could enact a scene showing primitive people trying to push a boulder in front of their cave opening for protection. They could then move the boulder by placing a strong branch (lever) under the boulder.   Explanation should point to the fact that the lever permits them to exert more force.

3.   Wheel and axle - Children could demonstrate the primitive method of moving loads by rolling logs under the loads. This "prewheel" and axle was inefficient, but it should be explained to the children that it was once the only method of moving a heavy load over a distance.

4.   Inclined plane - Children could enact a scene showing the ancient Egyptians building their pyramids by pushing heavy stone pieces up inclined planes. As an aid to this scene, illustrations of the pyramids should be displayed so the class can judge the enormity of the task of building the pyramids with only manual labor. Question: Could the pyramids have been built without the use of the inclined plane?

5.   Screw - Children could either enact or display illustrations of the Hanging Gardens of Babylon. The gardens were irrigated by means of huge turning screws which lifted water from the Euphrates River to the gardens. They could tell the story of King Nebuchadnezzar and his mountain princess and why the hanging gardens were built. It should be noted that the Hanging Gardens of Babylon are one of the wonders of the ancient world. Question: Can you think of another way the gardens could have been irrigated? Who do you suppose turned the giant screws?

6.   Pulley - Children could move almost to the present to enact a scene showing Francis Scott Key watching the raising of the flag at Fort McHenry during the War of 1812.

7.   Combine machines to show more complex developments. One combination of three simple machines was probably used in the construction of the pyramids. An inclined plane, log rollers (the wheel) and the pulley (or multiple pulley?) were probably combined in order to lift stones weighing many tons from ground level up to their proper positions. (See Fig. 10-9)

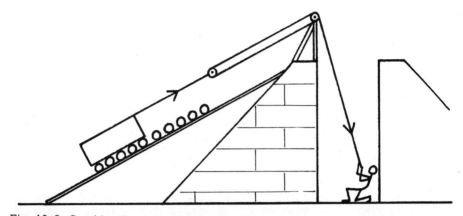

Fig. 10-9 Combination of Simple Machines.   This illustration shows the inclined plane, the wheel (log rollers), and the multiple pulley used to move a heavy stone as the pyramid builders may have done.   (James Thorpe)

Children could research to find out what combinations of this kind can be discovered locally.

To develop the concept of the machine age, each group could select an important invention to describe for the class. Each group would also mark on the time line the date of the invention. The class will observe that inventions of important machines cluster at the end of the time line marked "present." It should be explained that if they had lived only a few hundred years earlier, most machines would not have been invented yet. Inventions of important machines which children might select to describe include the printing press, the automobile, the airplane, the atomic reactor, and the cotton gin. Descriptions should include recognition of the various simple machines which are present within the complex machines.

Additional activities which could be used throughout the study include:

1.   Show filmstrips on simple machines.

2.   Have a child research and demonstrate the principle of the ball bearing.

3.   Have a child research and report on why the wheel is considered to be one of the most important inventions of all time.

4.   Hold a contest to see which child can locate, define, and explain the greatest number of simple machines within the classroom.   This would include such items as staplers, pencils, pencil sharpeners, scissors, doorknobs, drapery pulls, etc.

Books and magazines on simple machines should be available in the classroom for children who want to do additional reading. At the completion of the study, the children should have a better understanding of what the six simple machines are, how they function to make work easier, and an intuitive realization that machines exist all around us and influence nearly every aspect of life.

11 A Kernel Design on Transportation

Nature. . . doth teach us all to have aspiring minds. . . and measure every wandering planet's course. . . .

Christopher Marlowe

While it has been estimated that man has been around for more than half a million years, it is interesting to note that only in the last hundred years has man increased his average speed of travel over one thousand times and the average load he can transport over one million times. From the horse to Apollo, from the earliest backpack to the 50,000-ton supertanker, man's ability to move and to transport his possessions or his commerce have expanded more in the last hundred years than in the several hundred thousand years preceding them.

Even before his knowledge projected man into the machine age, he was a traveler, nomadic to a large extent. That man populated nearly every corner of the planet even before the machine age is tribute not only to his prolific reproduction but also to his basic need to move, whether for food or for space.

This kind of concept of time, of distance, or of progress, is very difficult for young children to grasp. This chapter shows how the kernel design can be used to help elementary school children understand and appreciate the historical development of overland transportation in the United States. It also explores the relationship between economic trends and the trucking industry.

NARRATIVE STATEMENT

The earliest form of transportation, of course, was walking. While man was well suited to carry light loads, he soon found he could move larger loads by using animals. He devised sleds and travois, again increasing the capacity of the load. As a result of these inventions, roads became desirable. Animal tracks which had been followed through forests or mountains were the primitive trails over which roads were laid. Once roads were developed, trading became a common activity. Settlements sprang up near river crossings and most communities became linked by roads.

Improvement in transportation increased through the years as efforts were made to better meet man's needs. Wells Fargo and Pony Express opened up vast territories. H. G. Wells once said, "Transportation and communication are the arteries and lifeblood of civilization." The Conestoga wagon was constructed to meet the specific needs of farmers in the Conestoga Valley of Pennsylvania. They needed tools, tea, sugar, and cloth in trade for their grain. The pack trains couldn't carry enough; most wagons couldn't use the trail, which was too mountainous and muddy. So the farmers, who were wagonbuilders from Germany, designed a wagon with a curved bed, slanted ends, and a white canvas cover held up by curved hoops. The driver walked along, holding one rein and guiding the team of horses.

These colorful red, white, and blue wagons originally traveled between Lancaster and Philadelphia. They were purchased by General Braddock in 1755 to haul supplies for the British over the Allegheny Mountains to Fort Duquesne on the Ohio River. A road had to be built for this purpose. Later, Fort Duquesne became Pittsburgh and many wagons traveled Braddock's road to the west. Today this road is called the National Road. It leads from Cumberland, Maryland to Wheeling, West Virginia. The road was narrow, bumpy, and muddy; in spots, the "corduroy road," logs laid side by side, improved and preserved the roadway. In 1792 the Philadelphia and Lancaster Turnpike Company was formed. The company hired a man named McAdam to build a two-lane highway. He used a roadbed of earth with broken rock rolled on top and covered with asphalt and tar or oil. The McAdam road was not only a giant stride into the future for transportation, but it resulted in more than one innovation of debatable value, among them the toll gate.

No new Conestoga wagons were built after the Erie Canal. Steam engines were designed for railroads, and they soon rendered the Conestoga wagons obsolete. However, their counterparts, the prairie schooners, served to carry pioneers across Indiana and Illinois. These were larger wagons, able to haul three or four tons and measuring 10 feet tall and over 20 feet long. The covered wagons of Kansas, Colorado, and the West Coast were still another style. They were lighter, shallower, flat-bottomed and included a driver's seat.

The need to save time and energy led to much progress in transportation, as did the discovery of various sources of power. The use of steam in Savery's vacuum led Newcomen to use a piston inside a cylinder to make a pump. Watt invented a piston that pushed up and down. He linked it to wheels, causing them to turn, thus giving power to sawmills. Cugnot, in 1769, invented a steampowered carriage in France. Trevithick, in 1804, invented a steam locomotive that could carry a 10-ton load on rails.

As inventions changed the means of transportation, so, too, they changed man's life. The Union Pacific Railroad spanned the continent, uniting East and West. The internal combustion engine, good steel, petroleum and the genius of men like Henry Ford all led to the mass production of automobiles. Family life, eating habits, vacations, vocations, and vocabularies reflected these changes.

In 1899, six hundred cars had been built in America. By 1925, there were

20 million! Cars influenced the rise of motels, fuel stations, factories, and traffic jams. They led to road signs, parking lots, junkyards, buses, trucks, and heavy daily doses of unburned hydrocarbons. Trucks improved our way of life by making more commodities available, creating more jobs and improving communication while also contributing to everything from malodorous streets to major issues in foreign policy.

Modern-day trucking is regulated by the Interstate Commerce Commission (I C C). The trucking industry must meet the contracts it signs with the powerful Teamsters' Union. "Tandems," "piggy-backs," "sleeper-cabs," and containerization are some of the more recent innovations of the trucking industry. The use of citizen-band radios is widespread in trucks today.

RESEARCHING ILLUSTRATIONS

In addition to history books, social studies textbooks, and encyclopedias, most state truckline associations have pictorial and printed materials available for public relations and educational purposes. A list of free resources and materials related to transportation has been supplied by the American Trucking Association. (See source materials at the end of this chapter.)

KERNELIZING THE HISTORICAL DEVELOPMENT OF TRANSPORTATION

Visually contrasting the Conestoga wagon to today's "eighteen-wheeler" can help students experience the concept of time and progress in overland transportation. A Conestoga wagon could be constructed using a long table with a stiff wire frame covered by a bed sheet. (See Fig. 11-1.)

Old wagon wheels from a farm could be wired to the legs on one side. Straw could form a sleeping mat. A "television screen" could be constructed and positioned so that anyone seated in the wagon can observe the "passing scene," that is, a moving mural of people, places, and things one might have observed while riding in a Conestoga wagon. This would be sturdier if done in a corner against two walls. A stepstool could be placed for easier boarding, and a child could actually take a turn riding as another child shows the artwork on the screen and narrates the passing scene. The "cargo" could include burlap sacks of grain, tools, and other primitive items.

In contrast to the Conestoga wagon, modern transport might be kernelized by the cab of an "eighteen-wheeler," accompanied by a "passing-scene" display. The passing scene could be coordinated with a tape of highway sounds that one might hear today. (See Fig. 11-2.)

Detailed directions for the construction of the truck cab are included in Chapter 12.

Within these two contrasting scenes of the Conestoga wagon and the truck cab, bulletin boards, blackboard, and seating arrangements can be altered to reflect the historical development of transportation. A busy street scene or expressway could be simulated on one side of the classroom; a mountainous, wooded area could be simulated on the other side. The general feeling of reality can be achieved through role-playing and heightened by sound effects. Like the scenographic elements which support the actor in his efforts on the stage, the kernelized concept of contrasting the Conestoga wagon to the "eighteen-wheeler" can stimulate children to research, recall, and relive the development of transportation, as well as relate it to man's dependence upon trucking today.

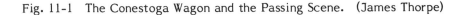

Fig. 11-1   The Conestoga Wagon and the Passing Scene.   (James Thorpe)

SMALL-GROUP RESEARCH ACTIVITIES

Numerous activities can be designed to help students gain a better concept of time and progress in overland transportation.   Samples of activities include the following:

1.   A group of students could put together the show or "passing scene" to be watched from the Conestoga wagon; another group could develop the "passing scene" to be watched from a modern-day truck.

2.   Discuss slogans and clichés about transportation. Is the quotation "bigger is better" a valid statement? Does saving time mean saving money? Do trucks really tear up the road? Are truck drivers the "knights of the highway" or "roadhogs?" One slogan of the trucking industry is, "If you got it, a truck brought it!" Is this always true? Have students research other transportation slogans.

3.   Have children divided into two groups.   One group creates a village as viewed during the days when the Conestoga wagon was the principal means of transportation; the other group designs a modern city. By building a town of houses, stores, factories, gas stations, and

schools the children will play in a creative environment and experience some of the principles of progress which would be too abstract for them to just read. Children need no prompting to play when there are cars or trucks around. They will "rev" the motors, back up, honk, speed down the highway on an errand of mercy, have a wreck, and "save the day" all in the span of 15 minutes.

4. Have the children graph the trucks they see in a week's time. They could graph the kind of truck, the product being transported, the license plate, and the direction (guess the destination) of travel.

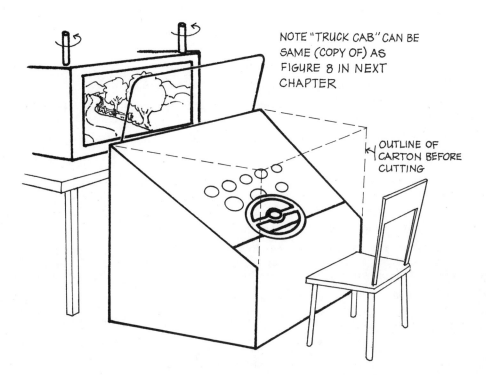

NOTE "TRUCK CAB" CAN BE SAME (COPY OF) AS FIGURE 8 IN NEXT CHAPTER

OUTLINE OF CARTON BEFORE CUTTING

Fig. 11-2   Truck Cab and the Passing Scene.   (James Thorpe)

5. Have children plan a trip on the national highways. List the towns, states, historical sites, and distances. Estimate the amount of fuel needed for a trip of this kind and compute the travel cost for various types of vehicles.

6. Drawings of highway signs could be made and their purpose discussed. If the classroom is designed to simulate the expressway

and/or busy intersections, the children could decide the appropriate places for the traffic signs. If possible, they could do this in the halls of the school or even on the playground areas.

7.   A dictionary of trucking terms could be made as a class project.

8.   The children could use a laminated map to draw in the early trails followed by settlers; using another colored pen, they could trace modern routes over these.

9.   Check labels on food and see from what state they came. On a large map, make string lines from the points of location to the students' hometown. A laminated map on which magic markers can be used to show locations is ideal for this activity.

10. Have a "design-a-car-for-the-future" contest. Voting should be based on the ideas used, not the art work.

11. Construct a simple steam engine and a pump.

12. Diagram or model an internal combustion engine.

13. Do experiments with the forces of gravity and friction. (See Chapter 10.)

14. Study why things float (density) and the effects of wind on a sail.

15. Use a tachometer and pedometer.

16. Make a chart comparing the top speed of man, animals, and various vehicles. Another chart could compare the size of the average load each can carry.

17. Visit a weigh station, a travel bureau, and a truck terminal.

18. Invite a truck driver to bring his truck to school. Let children sit in the cab and ask questions, see his log, hear the citizen's-band radio, and talk about safety, training, problems, and salary.

19. Visit a train-o-rama or set up a model train.

20. Try carrying loads using different means of transportation. Evaluate the best way.

21. Play "creative olympics." One at a time, each child goes across the gym in a different way - no two alike. Compare method and graph the times involved.

22. Have a toll gate and require "tickets" to use a certain part of the room. Offer transport services to principal, music teacher, cooks, and other school personnel. Stress prompt, dependable, quick, and safe service.

23. Act out the discovery of the wheel.

24. Have children write a story on the problems developing during a truck strike. This should lead to a greater understanding of man's dependence on the trucking industry and how the trucks play a vital role in even a child's life.

25. Have children research the relationship between trends in economics and the trucking industry.

26. With a fish market, butchershop, bakery, drugstore, hardware, and dimestore all in one, the modern supermarket is a shopper's paradise. Have students contrast the shopper of yesterday with the shopper today. Have them trace the influence that technological advances in refrigerated trucks and new insulated trailers have made in the shopping habits and menus of American families.

27. Using the Yellow Pages of a telephone directory, have the students list the services available today because of the trucking industry. Have them check those services which were not available 25 or 50 years ago.

28. Set up a travel bureau in the classroom. Pictures, folders, and brochures with the appropriate travel prices could be obtained from the AAA. Students could compare the cost of travel by plane with that of land travel. A debate on the advantages and disadvantages of specific forms of travel could be conducted.

29. As quoted in the narrative statement, H. G. Wells once said, "Transportation and communication are the arteries and lifeblood of civilization." Have students research and verify this statement.

SUMMARY

A process approach to learning transportation may be perceived as more time-consuming than a more traditional book-oriented approach; if, however, learning is more than just listening and remembering, then time has new meaning. These activities lead to a greater appreciation of the contributions the trucking industry has made to the development of new industries and the expansion of others. The activities also develop an awareness of the importance of trucking to the interdependence of people through the distribution of goods and services.

SOURCES OF FREE RESOURCE MATERIAL ON TRANSPORTATION*

Air Transport Associations
1709 New York Avenue, N.W.
Washington, D.C. 20006

American Association of State Highway Officials
National Press Building
Washington, D.C. 20004

American Trucking Associations, Inc.
1616 P Street, N.W.
Washington, D.C. 20036
Mr. J. R. Halladay, Vice President
Public and Industry Relations
   Telephone: (202) 797-5217

American Waterways Operators, Inc.
1250 Connecticut Avenue, N.W.
Washington, D.C. 20036

Association of American Railroads
1920 L Street, N.W.
Washington, D.C. 20036

Chamber of Commerce of the United States
1615 H Street, N.W.
Washington, D.C. 20006

Civil Aeronautics Board
1825 Connecticut Avenue, N.W.
Washington, D.C. 20428

Department of Transportation
400 7th Street, S.W.
Washington, D.C. 20590
(Office of the Secretary)
H. David Crowther,
Director of Public Affairs
Telephone: (202) 426-4570

Bureau of Motor Carrier Safety
(FHWA)
Werner A. Siems,
Director of Public Information
Telephone: (202) 426-0648

Federal Highway Administration
Werner A. Siems,
Director of Public Affairs
Telephone: (202) 426-4570

Federal Railroad Administration
Chris Knapton,
Public Affairs Officer
Telephone: (202) 426-0881

National Highway Traffic Safety Administration
B.A. Boaz,
Chief of Public Information
Telephone: (202) 426-9550

National Transportation Safety Board
Edward E. Slattery, Jr.,
Director of Public Information
Telephone: (202) 426-8787

Federal Maritime Commission
1405 I Street, N.W.
Washington, D.C. 20573

Highway Users Federation
1776 Massachusetts Avenue, N.W.
Washington, D.C. 20036

International Brotherhood of Teamsters
25 Louisiana Avenue, N.W.
Washington, D.C. 20001

Interstate Commerce Commission
12th Street and Constitution Avenue, N.W.
Washington, D.C. 20423

Motor Vehicle Manufacturers Association of the United States
1619 Massachusetts Avenue, N.W.
Washington, D.C. 20036
Oscar Griffin,
Director of Public Relations
Telephone: (202) 872-9339

National Association of Truck Stop Operators
501 Slaters Lane
Alexandria, Va. 22314

National Defense Transportation Association
1612 K. Street, N.W. No. 706
Washington, D.C. 20006

National Safety Council
425 North Michigan Avenue
Chicago, Illinois 60611

Transportation Association of
America
1101 17th Street, N.W.
Washington, D.C. 20036

Truck Trailer Manufacturers
Association
2430 Pennsylvania Avenue, N.W.
Washington, D.C. 20036
Charles J. Calvin,
Managing Director
Telephone: (202) 785-5833

Trucking Employees Inc.
1150 17th Street, N.W.
Washington, D.C. 20036

Western Highway Institute
333 Pine Street
San Francisco, Cal. 94104
Jess N. Rosenberg, Executive
Director
Telephone: (415) 986-4070

* Resource lists supplied by the American Trucking Associations, Inc.

SUPPLEMENTARY BIBLIOGRAPHY

Kohn, Bernice. Look-it-up book of transportation. New York: Random
House, 1968.

Lee and Lambert. The wonderful world of transportation. New York:
Garden City Books, 1960.

Maginely, C. J. Models of America's past and how to make them. New York:
Harcourt, Brace & World, 1969.

Richards, Kenneth. The story of the Conestoga wagon. Chicago: Children's
Press, 1970.

Sullivan, George. How does it get there?. Philadelphia: Westminster Press,
1973.

Tunis, Edwin. Tavern at the ferry. New York: Thomas Y. Crowell, 1973.

12 The Art and Craft of Kernelizing

"Simplify, simplify. Instead of three meals a day, if it be necessary eat but one; instead of a hundred dishes, five; and reduce other things in proportion" (p. 62). These words from Thoreau at Walden Pond should be your guide, for the primary keys to a creative classroom environment are simplicity, flexibility, and enrichment. The need for flexibility is underscored by Pumerantz, Howell, and Galano (1974), who state:

> The open environment for learning must be supported by a physical space design that is undefined and flexible so that instruction can focus on individual pupils and can support the integration of different learning experiences. The breakdown of walls and the opening up physically of the plant by itself does not guarantee an open environment. Altering physical space needs to be accompanied by an alteration of teaching and learning approaches. (p. 147)

According to Berger and Winters (1973), enrichment is a move away from the teacher-centered learning experience:

> The enriched environment of the open classroom is ideal for the development and possible solution of all kinds of problems. Without suggestions from you (the teacher), many problem-solving situations result simply from the social atmosphere in the room and the presence of many curiosity-stimulating materials. Problem-solving should emphasize the fact that learning is not a teacher-centered operation, but the result of searching for answers from many sources, especially personal experiences. (pp. 63-64)

An enriched environment, with great flexibility, designed to meet the learning needs of students in any social studies-centered unit, is provided by the simplified scenographic kernel design concept. It has been effectively proved that a social studies kernel design can be accomplished in the "average" classroom by a teacher unfamiliar with stage-craft techniques or without great skills as a craftsman. Both in-service teachers and preservice education students have implemented such study units for college class projects. Many of these projects have been used in both the elementary classroom and the junior high school. We assure you that it is not difficult.

VISUALIZING THE KERNEL

To some extent, the amount of space available for each element of a creative environment is irrelevant, for any scenic place may be scaled to fit any part of the classroom. This is not to say that space allocation is unimportant, but our major concerns at this point are the selection of a kernel and the mechanics of simplifying and crafting it. We have found that simply perusing a large number of illustrations will not quickly result in a suitable kernel. A trick often found useful is the use of the cardboard tube from a roll of toilet paper or paper toweling. Observe the whole illustration with one eye while viewing smaller portions through the tube. With a little practice, you will be able to retain a binocular view while concentrating on a small detail. In this way, the evocative impact of the detail may be analyzed effectively.

Too small a detail from the total illustration may not provide a useful kernel. Remember, the impact of the finished environment must be immediate and lasting, not for you but for small children. Too large a part of the whole is also to be avoided, although this error is less damaging, for it may be scaled down in size to fit anywhere. Even small children, however, may find ludicrous or ineffective a tiny version of a grand building; such kernels should be at least large enough to be imagined play-house size by the class. A door, for example, should be large enough, even if only implicitly to admit a real-life child.

Try projecting your illustration and your circled kernel on a blank wall before attempting to craft the item. It is usually helpful to view the whole picture and then select the many possible kernels in a size more appropriate for use. This will also often reveal details either desirable or too difficult for execution by your class. The opaque projector works well, both for such review and for the final drafting of a kernel design. Slides and the overhead projector, however, can also be used.

The art of kernelizing is really the art of visualizing and simplifying, and while mechanical aids are available to help you, your best tools are intuition, a keen eye for space, and a good narrative statement (your lesson plan). At times, the children can also assist in the process of kernelizing. According to Bremer and Bremer (1972):

> Young children are very good at creating habitats. Given a typewriter, a six year old will play office for hours . . . An old stethescope provokes an elaborate hospital game. Bits of wood and an iron bar in the backyard become a building site, a city block, gang territory.
> (p. 80)

A very instructive experiment in the process of kernelization would be to use the class as a jury to determine if the kernel is truly evocative. Pick a typical illustration, mask with plain paper all parts but a possible kernel and project it on a screen or wall. Ask your class to respond to what they see as they view the kernel first and then, progressively, the whole illustration. This can be a most enjoyable experiment and an effective way to kernelize.

Of some concern is the classroom itself and the total space available to you for decorative efforts. According to Spodek (1972), "it is important that teachers realize that the test of a good room arrangement is the degree to which it helps children achieve the goals of the program" (p. 238). If your classroom is of average size and over a few years old, you shouldn't be surprised to note that over 30 percent of the total volume of that room is wasted. Even with ample adult headroom, up to 5,000 cubic feet of space is available to the ceiling in a room only 35 feet square. This is one reason for advocating suspending kernel designs from the ceiling.

"The teacher must know how to arrange the physical environment and most importantly how to provision for it" (Pumerantz, Howell & Galano, 1974, p. 22). Space planning, not only for the creative environments but for seating arrangements and room for activity centers, will be facilitated by the use of a ground plan. The scaled ground plan sounds formidable, but it is a valuable aid and quite simple to construct and use. Scaled cutouts, representing the desks, movable furniture, and the kernel design constructions can be manipulated in many different positions on the ground plan without actually using one's physical energy to experiment. You may prefer laminating the ground plan and using a grease pencil to plan the physical arrangement. The ground plan of your room will show the floor and walls in section, with important elements such as doors or windows or items which descend from the walls in exact lateral relationship. The sample ground plan displayed in Fig. 12-1, shows a classroom 30 feet by 20 feet.

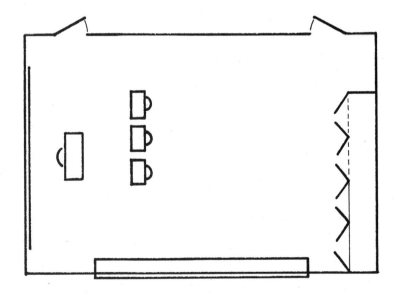

Fig. 12-1 Sample Groundplan (James Thorpe)

The scale, not precise in so small an example, is 1/8 inch : 1 foot. The plan shows two doors, a closet with four openings, a window 18 feet long with a radiator below, and some desks and chairs. The only thing a ground plan does not precisely show is the vertical dimension of any object. To execute the scaled ground plan, you first select a scale, or ratio of size. For example, if your classroom is 30 feet square, in a scale of 1 inch = 1 foot, your ground plan will be 30 inches (plus some margin) square. This may be about right, or it may seem a bit unwieldy, especially if it is dry mounted or laminated. The usual scale increment is 1/4 inch, so the next smaller scale, 3/4 inch : 1 foot, would result in a ground plan 26 1/4 inches square. While the architect's scale is the preferred tool for measuring in scale, the acceptable scales are such that a one-foot standard ruler will be easy enough to use.

CARDBOARD: THE CORE OF KERNEL DESIGN CONSTRUCTIONS

Since cardboard is the most commonly used material in constructing kernel designs, this section presents some very practical suggestions regarding its use. Cardboard does some things very well but fails miserably when mishandled. Fig. 12-2 shows a cutaway view of the three plies of corrugated cardboard.

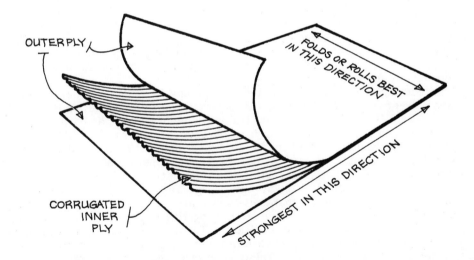

Fig. 12-2 Corrugated Cardboard Cutaway (James Thorpe)

It is best to fold or roll <u>across</u> the inner ply, or to make the direction of the inner ply provide for strength in large pieces. Three-ply corrugated cardboard is fairly strong <u>along</u> the line of the inner or corrugated ply. It is quite flexible, and therefore quite weak, <u>across</u> that inner ply. Corrugated cardboard may not be self-supporting when used in large sheets with no folds. It may warp when left suspended or standing in a place where humidity is high. This could be true of any classroom without air conditioning. It may delaminate, or come apart into three separate layers if soaked with paint as well as with plain water.

Some of the distinctive advantages of cardboard are: it is usually free; it takes paint well in very thin coats; it may be scored and folded as well as cut and reglued; it is very light in weight (a boon when suspended scenic pieces are mandated by lack of classroom space); it is relatively easy to cut with a knife; and it may be bent, folded, curled, or otherwise easily manipulated by small hands.

Some helpful hints for cutting corrugated cardboard include the following. If the piece is to be folded or assembled and is not two-dimensional, plan your cuts or folds by making a paper model. Use a straight edge with a metal edge if possible. Place something, wood preferably, under your cut line. A utility knife blade will make quite a mess of a table top, a desk top, or even a vinyl floor. Plan your cuts of assembly so that the largest dimension is <u>along</u> the line of corrugation where the greatest strength lies. In this way you may avoid the necessity of battening, or stiffening. Don't be afraid of three-dimensional units. Even a very shallow thickness piece, especially on curved lines, can be effective in both stiffening a large piece and in adding to the illusion of reality.

It will be an almost irresistible temptation to use free, easily accessible materials like refrigerator or stove cartons to create three-dimensional playhouse kernels. While we have observed very successful reading centers, for example, made of a large carton and providing a quiet, cozy, private study area, even these usually are thrown away to make room for other functions. The ideal kernel should be constructed so that it can be folded and stored economically for future use.

In teaching stagecraft and theater scenography for many years, one of the authors eventually learned to cope with a hard lesson: Simplification is much, much more difficult than imitation. If this is true of people who have already chosen a highly technical and artistic avenue of expression such as the theater, how could it be otherwise for most teachers? It is, then, very natural - predictable in fact - that the three-dimensional, "naturalistic" center will appear and disappear with some regularity.

Let's take a practical look at our refrigerator carton. With a bit of planning, that three-dimensional, self-supporting carton may be cut, scored, folded, and lightly taped to remain self-supporting while folding for storage into an essentially two-dimensional unit. To illustrate this point, detailed step-by-step instructions for constructing the cab of a truck, referred to in Chapter 11, are included here. These same principles can be applied to the construction of numerous kernel designs using a cardboard carton as a base.

The construction of a truck cab is one of the few cases in which the raw material, the box, needs to be of a specific size or minimum size. Base your dimensions on the height of a classroom chair suitable for your average pupil - this should range from 14 inches to 16 inches from floor to seat. The "dashboard" of the truck should be a slanted surface easily observed by a comfortably seated child. A box measuring at least 36 inches wide by 8 inches deep by 30 inches high will do nicely.

Set up the box and mark for cutting as shown in Figs. 12-3 through 12-8.

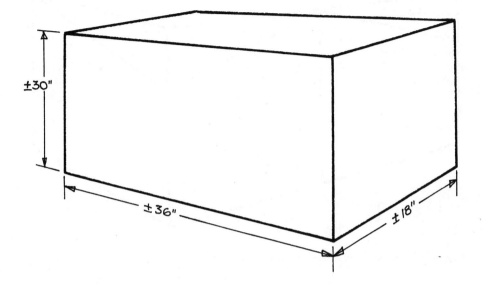

Fig. 12-3   Set-up   (James Thorpe)

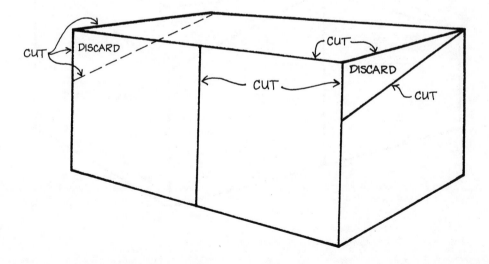

Fig. 12-4   Primary Cuts   (James Thorpe)

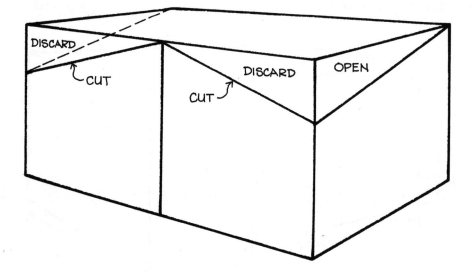

Fig. 12-5   Secondary Cuts   (James Thorpe)

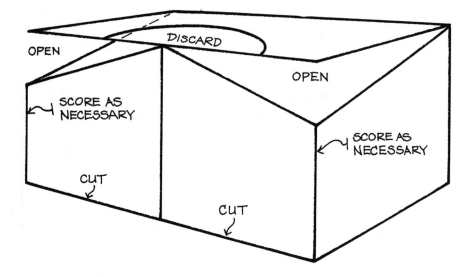

Fig. 12-6   Final Cuts   (James Thorpe)

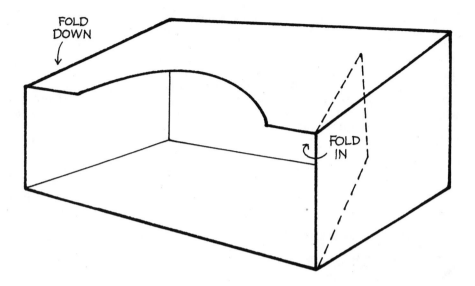

Fig. 12-7   Folding   (James Thorpe)

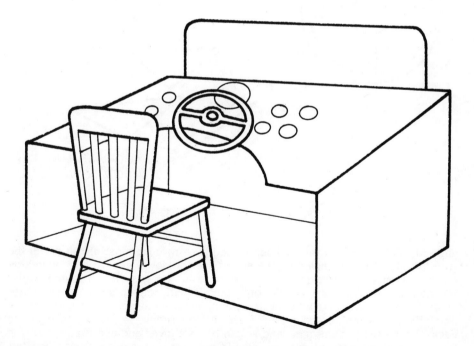

Fig. 12-8   Completing the Details   (James Thorpe)

Remember, some of the cuts must be made through only one layer of the three-dimensional cardboard. These score cuts are to facilitate folding. Use a straight edge (preferably of metal or metal-edged) whenever possible, especially for score cuts. A crooked score will not fold easily, if it folds at all.

Use a piece of soft wire and bend a windshield frame (the wire may be punched through the cardboard dashboard where it looks best). Paint on gauges of various sorts. If you can integrate science or math activities using concepts such as speed and distance or miles per gallon, each appropriate gauge may be made functional by adding a heavy paper "needle" affixed with a brad.

If you can locate a relatively large light plastic steering wheel from a child's toy, you can mount it in various ways so as to be practical. One method is illustrated in Fig. 12-9. Fix the dowel to the steering wheel with a

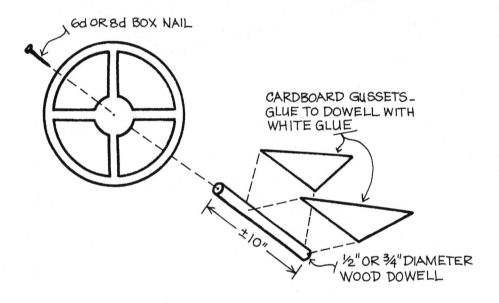

Fig. 12-9   Mounting the Steering Wheel   (James Thorpe)

nail, cut a hole through the dashboard, and push through most of the dowel (be sure the wheel still turns), glue the gussets to the dowel and to the underside of the dashboard. Use masking tape to hold the gussets in place while the glue dries. This practical scenic device will help to set an appropriate mood for the study of transportation, and, when no longer needed, it may be partially disassembled and folded flat. It will require a bit of space in the back of a closet for storage, and it can be used over and over again. This is but a single example of why we should not just use the cardboard box but consider it the raw material of a scenic or practical kernel design.

THE CRAFT OF KERNELIZING

"Materials in the open classroom provide the structure. The sequencing of materials must be thoroughly understood by the teacher if she is to understand how children can interact with the materials to learn" (Pumerantz, Howell, & Galano, p. 22).   Marsh (1970) also emphasizes the teacher's role in maximizing the potential of materials:

> . . . the control of raw materials becomes a highly significant and selective influence at the command of the teacher.   The choices exercised by the teacher in relation to materials and starting-points are a positive influence and lead to a weighting of situations that cause children to experience a sensually appreciated small-scale environment ('seeing the wood by means of the trees') and the reflective feeling response to the world. It is of a different kind to the series of rote items in the instruction-based curriculum of the old elementary school. It reveals a view of people as people and not as instruments of the emerging industrially and commercially based society.
> (p. 127)

Experience with preservice and in-service teachers has revealed a need for assistance and practical suggestions for using materials and tools.   This section includes suggestions for the physical construction of kernels suggested in the book or common kernel designs that teachers have tried in their classrooms.

Construction of a log house

In Chapter 5, you saw the need for a log house. The utilitarian nature of the log house contributed to its popularity in our frontier development, and examples of many styles remain today.   The design of a log house is, therefore, no problem - it is the kernel which may be surprisingly difficult. Again, the difficulty encountered is often based upon the question of how to simplify.

Since pioneer and Indian units are part of every social studies curriculum, and since they represent a relatively easy way to study the concept of community and to involve children in role-playing situations, we have seen quite a number of preservice and in-service teachers' efforts at such a creative atmosphere. We will discuss in more detail here two of the most divergent approaches teachers used to develop this kernel.

One version of a log cabin was constructed with carpet rolls, heavy cardboard tubes from three to four inches in diameter upon which new carpeting is rolled for shipment and display. (See Fig. 12-10.)

Carpet rolls can usually be found free of cost in any community with a carpet store or major building supply house. Carpet rolls come in lengths up to 12 feet and are light in weight considering their strength. This log-cabin version also assumes a wood shop or industrial arts area in the school or in another nearby building in the system, where these rolls may be cut easily to

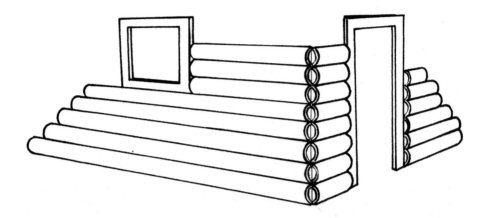

Fig. 12-10 Exterior View of the Log Cabin Built from Rug Roll Logs
(James Thorpe)

length and, using an industrial band saw, split down the center to form two equal half rolls. These halves are then glued to cardboard (perhaps lightly stiffened with wood) to form a cutaway, a realistic log house which is self-standing, but which will fold inward for storage. It will be a little thicker when folded than the total size of the original rug roll.

To construct the log cabin, cut to shape the sides of the log cabin, score, and hinge main piece of cardboard as illustrated in Fig. 12-11.

Make the door and window frames from cardboard as illustrated in Fig. 12-12. Hold them in place with masking tape and simply paint over the tape. Be certain to lay out and score cardboard for such units along the line of the inner corrugations. Greater strength will result, as well as easier scoring and folding.

An even simpler version of the construction of a log cabin is the same basic simplification, or kernel, cut with more detail from cardboard and painted to look like logs. Such a kernel need not be large. It can serve as an activity center for related activities or just reading if it gives the illusion of privacy. The addition of a door frame and a window covered with oiled paper aids in the illusion of reality and adds to the size of the piece without adding much weight or making it a permanent fixture.

Fig. 12-13 shows the interior view of the log cabin which could be used in both versions of the log cabin. The fireplace and mantel added in the drawings may be easily fabricated from one piece of cardboard if greater simplicity is desired. Use the same basic technique as described for the construction of door-window frames, beams, etc., and affix with masking tape. If the kernel may have to be moved or stored during the unit of study, use the "Tab A into slot B" technique. When cutting the fireplace, remember to cut so that two or more tabs up to 1 inch in depth are extended from each side.

Cut slots at the corresponding places on the inside wall of the kernel and

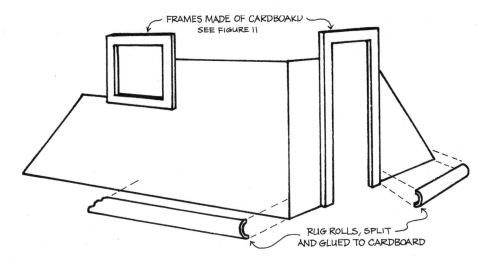

Fig. 12-11   Exploded View of Log Cabin.   Glue half-rolls to cardboard with white glue.   A few staples from the inside or masking tape from the outside will help hold rolls in place while the glue dries.   (James Thorpe)

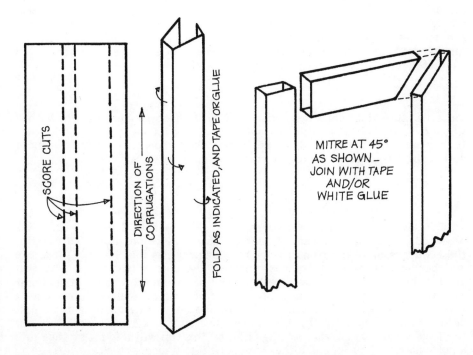

Fig. 12-12   Folded, Taped Cardboard Frames   (James Thorpe)

Fig. 12-13 Interior View of Log Cabin. Note that this kernel is made in a cutaway fashion, including a corner and an irregular part of two walls - the third and fourth walls are supplied by a corner of your classroom. This is a classic example of kernelizing. Only enough of the cabin is reproduced to conjure up the illusion of such a place. The imagination of your class will supply the missing parts of the walls, the practical door, the beams and roof and the other two walls. Compare this concept for flexibility with the "playhouse" unit, with bottom, top, and 4 sides, made of a refrigerator carton without modification.   (James Thorpe)

force-fit these tabs into the slots. For best effect, make the slot with a single cut, widen it a bit with sideways pressure of the knife blade, and force-fit the tab. In this fashion the fireplace may be temporarily removed without destroying a decorative job of painting by pulling off the tape.

Construction of a tipi

Cut seven to nine narrow wedges of cardboard about 8 inches across the base and as high as you want; 5 feet or more will be possible. Split one of these wedges to make two narrow right triangles. See Fig. 12-14. These two will be the first and last wedges, allowing the unit, when standing, to rest against the wall. Tape these together from base to apex, cut into the center whatever size entrance you want, and stand against the wall with the base in a semicircle. Greater realism can be obtained by taping eight to ten sticks onto the top to represent the tops of the tipi framework as they would project from the sewn hide cover. See Fig. 12-15. This tipi will fold for storage into a piece about 5 feet long, 8 inches wide, and 4 to 5 inches thick.

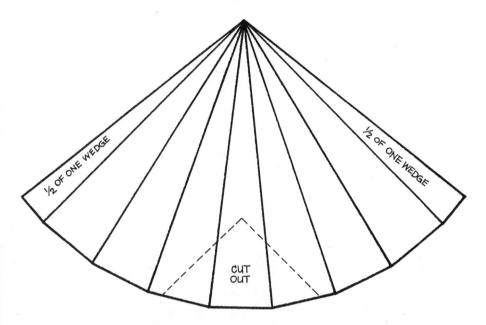

Fig. 12-14   The Tipi - Step 1   (James Thorpe)

Construction of a wishing well

Even simpler than a tipi, the wishing well, exemplary of a number of pieces, can be partially three-dimensional and partially two-dimensional and can be disassembled and stored. (See Fig. 12-16.)

Construct the well housing from a circle, cut in two equal parts. Cut a piece of cardboard as high as you wish the well housing to be, and equal in width (across the corrugations) to one-half the circumference of the original circle. One half circle is the base, the second half circle the top (cut it out a bit if you want to drop things into it). Tape these three pieces together on the inside, so your paint job won't be destroyed by disassembling, and stand the unit against a wall. The verticals, the roller and handle, and a roof if desired, can be two-dimensional and taped to the wall above the well housing.

Designing stained-glass windows

Make a cardboard frame, designed to be taped to a window frame or a small part of a window unit (the larger the better). Cut a large number of narrow cardboard strips   about 1/2 inch wide and of considerable length. Working on the floor from the back of the unit, lay out the larger areas of the window by gluing on these strips. Make a full-size pattern on newsprint or butcher paper to avoid mistakes. Use pieces of theatrical gelatin for the windows, overlapping each piece about 1/2 inch. Theatrical gelatin is exactly

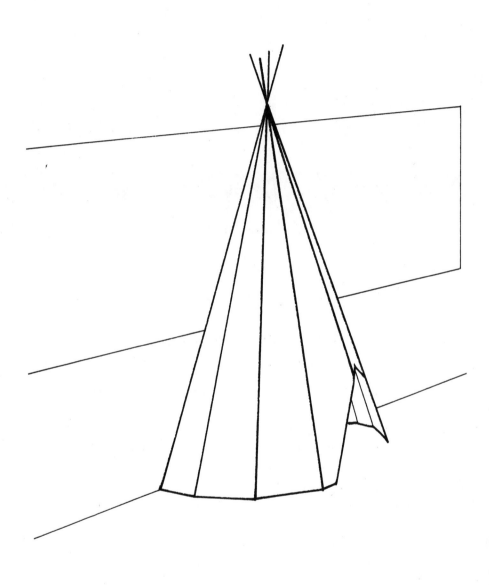

Fig. 12-15   The Tipi - Step 2   (James Thorpe)

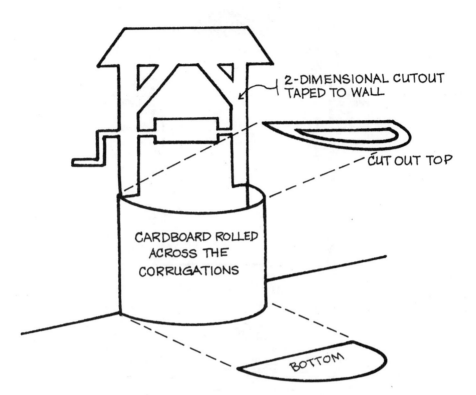

Fig. 12-16 A Wishing Well (James Thorpe)

what it sounds like, very thin sheets of gelatin, impregnated with dye for the color. Gelatin will dissolve, of course, so gently wetting the overlapped edges of any two pieces will partially dissolve them and "glue" them together as they dry. White glue will attach pieces to the main cardboard frames. The result will be transparent, as colorful and detailed as you wish, and very impressive when the sun shines through it. Note that many colors, in addition to those you can find in scraps from your local civic theater group, can be created by overlapping primary or secondary colors, a good introduction to the physics of color.

Modifying windows and doors

Often, furniture, doors, and windows already available in the classroom can be modified to create appropriate kernel designs. For example, one teacher used the playhouse already in the classroom and just attached the design of the pagoda roof to represent the Japanese home. A heavy quilt or sleeping bag was used for the bed. Following the customs of the Japanese,

Asian Gateway, c BC 1350. Classroom door opening is shown in broken line.

Georgian Doorway. Classroom door opening is shown in broken line.

Fig. 12-17 Examples of Doorway Kernels (James Thorpe)

Arch of Septimus Severus, Rome. Kernel classroom door opening is shown in broken line.

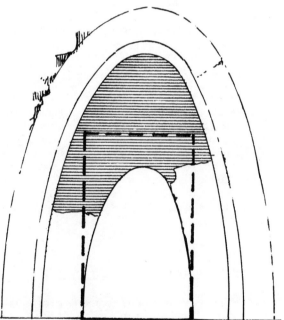

Assyrian Gateway. Classroom door opening is shown in broken line.

the children took off their shoes before entering the house and sat on the floor. It made an ideal reading center. In this same classroom, the art center was identified with screen painting on cardboard dividers to represent one of the many arts of Japan. Desks can also be modified to serve as kernel designs. One teacher, during a study on Holland, used desks as the base for windmills and kayaks. Cardboard and paper dikes and canals were used to divide the classroom into various learning centers.

With most kernels of architectural detail, it is the openings, their characteristic shape, decoration, or size, which make the best suggestive units. The approach also may have psychological implications for role-playing by your class. The doorway, both practically and symbolically, denies entry or admits one to new places and opportunities. While a kernel which is nothing but a wall may delineate an area of your room as a special place, entering that place through a doorway will make it much more believable.

There are practical advantages to the use of permanent features of your room such as doors or windows. Your decorative kernel need not, for example, be self-standing or self-supporting. The kernel also does not use any floor space; it need never be shifted out of the way to make room for another activity. Cardboard cutouts of characteristic period doors or windows, even quite large and detailed, may be fastened to existing frames with masking tape or double-faced carpet tape. When this approach is combined with suspended or self-standing pieces, appropriate implements, fragments of costume, and integrated displays of art, you will have created an atmosphere most convincing and still economical of space and materials. Examples of characteristic openings are illustrated in Fig. 12-17.

These typical illustrations are, of course, too small to use, but each of these, as well as literally hundreds more like them from all periods and geographical areas, are easily available in larger, clearer form, many in color. Some may be kernelized from the same or similar materials as the original, as in the case of the Hawaiian grass pavilion. Clearly, each of these illustrations and the hundreds of others you will be able to locate will be quite easy to construct, simply by adding distinctive shapes and details to a standard door. This basic, easy kernel design unit might be the first of a number of kernels for a study unit. Think of the surprise and the curiosity with which you will be greeted if you make such a kernel yourself, and have it in place on Monday morning, well in advance of the beginning of the study unit.

THE ART OF KERNELIZING

When the research for a creative environment is completed and a kernel or kernels are selected and transferred to cardboard or other material, a very enjoyable part of the process begins - painting, assembling, completing and displaying the pieces. Here are a few shortcuts and hints which might save you and your class a few false starts, corrections, or even the frustration of beginning again from the raw material.

Basic painting techniques

In nature (and you will use nature as a subject, though not so often as architecture) there are no lines. This means not just a dearth of straight lines, but no lines of any sort. What may appear to have to be drawn as a line is only the edge of one thing as perceived against a background of other things. What this means for you as a "scenic artist" is simply that brush strokes make better lines than ruled lines. Soft, irregular pencil lines will serve nicely to outline an object, but you should not actually paint in those lines. Rather, you should apply base color up to the line or even over it. Where a hard, distinct "line" is perceived as the edge of a nearby object, overlap the ground colors of the background object. Where a distant object is seen less distinctly, don't overlap the lines but lay in each line up to but not touching each other.

In nature, and in many architectural features, there is no such thing as a pure color or an object which is of a single color. Highlights and shadows alone change our perception of color. Distance apparently changes color, and nature herself supplies her creations with an infinite variety of subtle shadings.

To successfully paint your kernel, or to help your students discover and apply the details of paint, a few somewhat more practical hints might be remembered. Never try to cover an area with paint. Apply paint in most cases with a dry-brush technique. Successive applications of different colors for shading or natural variety will ultimately cover your cardboard model so that little or no cardboard is seen. Instead of heavy coats of paint, which are effective only when painting houses or barns or the like, apply the paint in light, uneven coats, allowing each coat to dry somewhat before the next color is applied. While the subtle blending that occurs when colors are built up wet may be desirable for some easel work, remember not to soak the cardboard, lest it collapses.

Children tend to draw detail before background if they include background at all. You must help them reverse this approach for scenic work. Applying fine detail over a series of groundcoats will keep your finished kernel from looking like a colored ditto done by "staying inside the lines." Another often unfortunate generalization is that because "children love bright colors" such work must be done in pure, exaggerated shades, or that shades of grey must not be used. You can aid the discovery process in small ways by encouraging closer analytical observation of real things in preparation for kernel work. Discuss your observations of color, perspective, shading, and other nuances, what they mean, and why they occur.

Adding to the illusion of size

Sophisticated adult theater audiences often have been deceived by a technique called "forced perspective." Perspective, simplified, is seen most clearly when looking at a large building. Note that the lines of the bottom and the roof (if flat) tend to converge somewhere beyond the end farthest from you. If those lines were extended far enough they would appear to meet at a single point on the horizon. Forcing perspective for scenic purposes means forcing those lines to converge more rapidly. The result will be a relatively short building which looks longer than it really is.

A method of forcing perspective for top lines is shown in Figs. 12-18 and 12-19. Note that the bottom line cannot be "forced." If it is forced, as is the top, the unit will no longer sit level on the floor. Fold the unit out flat. Draw a <u>light</u> line across it, (line A) parallel to the floor, at the average height

Fig. 12-18   A Sample Two-sided Playhouse Kernel   (James Thorpe)

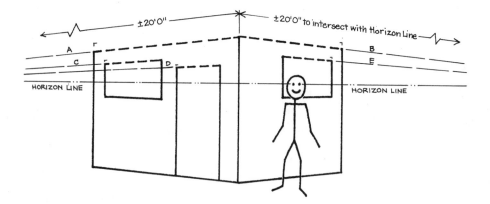

Fig. 12-19   Playhouse Kernel, Showing Elementary Forced Perspective Procedures. New, forced top lines are shown as broken lines. (James Thorpe)

of the eye of a standing student. This is his <u>horizon</u> <u>line</u>, somewhere on which, at infinity, top and bottom lines will normally appear to converge. Draw two tentative cut lines (lines A and B) from the fold or corner at the top of the unit so that if extended each of these cut lines will converge with the horizon at points equidistant and as far as possible from the top corner. Change each horizontal line, such as the tops of doors and windows (lines C, D, and E) above the forced horizon to converge, if extended, at the same points as A and B, and you will have made an arbitrary but effective change in perspective. From the child's-eye view this will make a small unit look somewhat deeper and larger than it really is. A hint: the vanishing points may be located and the lines to them drawn by using a piece of string about 15 to 20 feet long.

The nuts and bolts needed for constructing kernel designs

Most of the tools you will use to craft a creative classroom environment are already in your classroom. A few power tools may be helpful, but very little sophisticated equipment can even be justified. Tools can be classified into three categories: common tools for everyday use, power tools for more sophisticated techniques, and dangerous tools not likely to be used by very young students.

Common tools

<u>Scissors:</u> Shears is a better name. The little scissors used by primary pupils won't really cut most materials used in the crafting of a kernel.

<u>Glue:</u> A white glue, basically a protein product, is far superior to library paste, although mucilage is useful for small constructions.

<u>Masking tape:</u> A really basic tool and material which holds well on most paper products and which takes paint or tempera very well. Even painted, masking tape may usually be removed without damaging the material taped, and is very easy to use.

<u>Stapler:</u> A good-quality desk stapler (such as the Bates 500 series which easily opens to become a staple driver) is suggested. The disadvantage of this tool is in the shortness of the standard staple, which will not penetrate three-ply corrugated cardboard and a wood or other hard backing. However, such a tool is also easy to operate with small hands and is reasonably safe.

<u>Measuring tools:</u> Many types are available, and several should be made available, even if only occasionally used. They include: folding rule, 6 inches or 8 inches in length and also marked in metrics if possible; steel tape, 6 feet or 12 feet in length and also marked in metrics, if possible; tri-square, marked in inches; and a steel tape, 50 feet in length and also marked in metrics if possible.

The length of the steel tapes may seem excessive, but if your pupils are to fully participate in crafting a creative atmosphere, full-scale measurements of the classroom may often be needed. Further, very long measuring tools may be used to demonstrate, indoors or out, the actual size of many aspects of a kernel.

Sandpaper: For centuries, craftsmen have used something like our modern sandpaper to remove the "curse" from pieces of wood. Splinters are no fun, especially in little fingers, and some wood is often necessary to stiffen cardboard for architectural kernels.   Use the sandpaper on all edges and corners to make wood more pleasurable to handle.

Pliers: Electrician's pliers will also cut wire.

Screwdriver: for slot-head wood screws.

Hammer: Use the lightest you can get if you want your pupils to be effective in their early wood-joining efforts.

Wire: Light to medium annealed wire is very good, for it cuts easily, is very soft and easy to bend or twist, and is still reasonably strong. Annealed wire is available in spools of varying length, it is inexpensive and it may be reused successfully in many cases.

Yardstick: This is listed separately from measuring tools, because its suggested use is as a straight edge for drawing, marking, or cutting.

Power tools

Power drill: This is the only power tool really needed, and, if you are clever, you may even dispense with this tool. If a power drill is available, be sure to provide a reasonable variety of bits.   The best bits for your purposes are generally referred to as "speed-bore" bits.   They are for wood boring only; they are very fast and efficient; and they are available in small kits with sizes ranging from 1/8 inch to 1 inch in diameter.

Dangerous tools

Hand saw: The best general tool is a small cross-cut (not rip-tooth) hand saw. The number of teeth per inch and the set, or width of the teeth, determines the ability of the saw to cut across or with the grain. A short 16- to 18-inch saw with ten to twelve teeth per inch is preferred.

Knife: This is the most frequently used tool for manipulating cardboard. The utility knife or matte knife, with a retractable razor-like blade is the best and safest.

Scribe or compass: Something larger than the student compass, capable of inscribing a diameter of 10 to 12 inches.

Staple gun: Much more powerful than the desk stapler, the staple gun will drive a staple up to 5/8 inch in length into soft wood such as pine. While this tool is very useful for stiffening large pieces of cardboard by affixing battens to the back of the piece, it is also much more difficult to use and considerably more dangerous. We suggest that only the teacher use a staple gun.

Nails: Carpet tacks and 1-1/4 inch lath nails are usually all the sizes needed, as the average set piece is not weight-bearing.

Screws: Slot-head wood screws will be needed. We suggest 1-1/4 inch No. 8, and 5/8 inch No. 6 screws as useful sizes.

Fasteners: Other fasteners found useful include cup hooks, screen-door hooks, and eye sets, 1 inch or 1-1/2 inch loose-pin hinges, and small screw eyes.

Don't go out and buy all of these small items. We have found that most or all of the items are already available somewhere in every school building. Check with your custodian.

Materials

Nearly all of the items or pieces that can contribute to a creative atmosphere (other than assigned pupil projects in art) may be constructed of three-ply corrugated cardboard.   Useful additional materials are butcher paper (very sturdy) or a roll of newsprint (less sturdy, but usually a lot cheaper), and muslin (unbleached is best, but old bedsheets will suffice). With these materials, basic tools, and a well-planned unit, you will be surprised at the mood-setting or mood-heightening effects you will be able to create.

Muslin is a very valuable stagecraft material. It is very inexpensive; it is very easy to tear, cut, sew, or glue; it is surprisingly strong when stretched or framed; and it is a fine hinge when glued to cardboard. It may be made translucent or opaque, and is easy to paint, especially when presized with paste or glue. It is easy to store for reuse, and, unfortunately in a few cases, it is guaranteed to shrink. Unbleached muslin of a good grade will shrink up to three inches per yard. Actually, this is sometimes an advantage, for when the muslin is loosely laid on a frame and firmly stapled or glued, the application of a groundcoat of water-base paint will fill the pores of the cloth and shrink it tight on the frame, ready to use as a canvas.

This material comes with a selvage edge, a method of binding the edges to prevent raveling. Always remove this selvage; it does not shrink at the same rate as the body of the material. Tear, don't cut, unbleached muslin. Tearing in either direction is easy but more important, it leaves a "soft" edge and "feathers," or tends to disappear, when glued to wood or cardboard. Bleached muslin (bed sheets for example) is preshrunk. This muslin (unlike percale) is of a rather light grade and is less useful than unbleached muslin for most scenic purposes.

Muslin makes a good hinge for operational doors in architectural kernels. Apply a strip (a "dutchman" in theatrical parlance) about 2 to 3 inches wide with thinned white glue, or with a mixture of three to four parts wheat paste (wallpaper paste) to one part unthinned white glue. Apply the dutchman hinge on the same side as the direction of the swing of the door. When painted, a dutchman will essentially disappear.

Another valuable material is white glue. Some of its strengths are that it is strong, fast drying (on wood only 20 to 30 minutes are required for a good bond and much less time is required on paper, cardboard, or cloth); it is flexible, clear when dry, and cleanable (when still wet) with soap and water.

It is also thinable with water when a size coat is wanted, as in the use of muslin.

Your local civic theater may be able to lend you another mood-setting device, namely sound. Sound-effect records will often create a better atmosphere than visual effects. For example, storms, wind, and highway sounds may be extremely effective in contributing to the illusions created by a kernel. By dubbing selected effects onto cassettes you may reuse them with a kernel in the future.

SUMMARY

You will certainly encounter problems or questions not answered in this brief review of scenic techniques. We have not attempted to produce a complete stagecraft handbook as there are many good texts already available which can be helpful to you in your efforts to promote a creative classroom environment. Your own ingenuity will also help you. You will soon, with just a bit of cleverness and a lot of good planning, create illusions or creative atmospheres well beyond the scope of the examples we have provided.

Planning is the key word at this point. Since much of what we encourage is based on simplicity, some experiments may be necessary in order to find the simplest design and the simplest method. Try a version of the Oriental art of origami, or paperfolding. Make a small, preferably scaled version of any complex kernel in paper; plan your folds and cuts so that you won't make time-consuming mistakes when producing the finished item.

Above all, plan for simplicity so that your pupils can be involved. Simplify both for them (according to their level of manipulative skill) and for yourself to reduce the supervisory time and effort required to involve the class. When possible, write out directions for certain parts of the construction or finishing process, so that the children will benefit from practice in reading and following reasonably complex directions. Simplicity is further justified by the need to have fun in the process of building a creative classroom environment. If the process is too difficult, or if it takes too long to realize the finished product, children may lose interest before you get to the point at which you can actually use the kernels you have designed.

REFERENCES

Berger, E., and Winter, B.A. Social studies in the open classroom: A practical guide. New York: Teacher's College Press, 1973.

Bremer, A., and Bremer, T. Open education: A beginning. New York: Holt, Rinehart, & Winston, 1972.

Marsh, L. Alongside the child, experiences in the English primary school. New York: Harper & Row, 1970.

Pumerantz, P., Howell, B., and Galano, R.W. Administrator's guide to the open learning environment. New York: Parker, 1974.

Spodek, B. Teaching in the early years. Englewood Cliffs, N.J.: Prentice-Hall, 1972.

Thoreau, Henry David. Walden and civil disobedience, edited by Owen Thomas. New York: Norton, 1966.

SUPPLEMENTARY BIBLIOGRAPHY

Adix, V. Theater scenecraft. Children's Theater Press, 1956.

Bowman, N.A. A handbook of technical practice for the performing arts; in two parts. Wilkinsburg: Scenographic Media, 1972-1975.

Buerki, F.A. Stagecraft for nonprofessionals, 3rd ed. Boston: Little, Brown, 1972.

Gassner, J. Producing the play (with the new scene technician's handbook by Phillip Barber rev. ed. New York: Holt, Rinehart & Winston, 1965.

Gillette, A.S. An introduction to scenic design. New York: Harper & Row, 1967.

Gillette, A.S. Stage scenery: Its construction and rigging, 2nd ed. New York: Harper & Row, 1972.

Gruver, E.A. The stage manager's handbook. New York: DBS Publications, 1971.

Heffner, H. C. Modern theater practice, 4th ed. New York: Appleton-Century-Crofts, 1959.

International Theater Institution. Stage design throughout the world since 1950. New York: Theater Arts Books, 1964.

Stage design throughout the world since 1960. New York: Theater Arts Books, 1973.

Kenton, W. Stage properties and how to make them. New Rochelle, N.Y.: Soccer Associates, 1974.

Lounsbury, W.C. Theater backstage from A to Z. Seattle: University of Washington Press, 1967.

MacGowan, K. Continental Stagecraft. New York: Harcourt, Brace, 1922.

Parker, W.O. Scene design and stagelighting, 2nd ed. New York: Holt, Rinehart & Winston, 1968.

Pectal, L. Designing and painting for the theater. New York: Holt, Rinehart & Winston, 1975.

Simon, B., ed. Simon's directory, 4th ed. Washington, D.C.: American Theater Association, 1970.

Smith, M. Equipment of the school theater. (Reprint of the 1930 edition) New York: AMX Press, 1974.

Wilfred, T. Projected scenery: A technical manual. New York: Drama Book Specialists, 1965.

13 The Kernel Design: An Overview

The problem of education is to see the wood by means of the tree.
Alfred Whitehead (1929)

AN OVERVIEW

Commenting on Whitehead's statement, Marsh (1970) feels "it is this view that leads to an understanding of the sensually appreciated environment with the teacher's most important role that of heightening the <u>process</u> of sense impact" (p. 122). The creative classroom environment enhanced by the kernel design is rich in multisensory experiences. It is based on the conviction that "it is the task of education to enlarge the frontiers of children's experience in time and space and understanding" (Allen 1970, p. 231). According to Marsh, "the acceptance of the richness of any environment has a powerful consequence for our view of the curriculum and the opportunities given to children. The street, with its shadows, textures, sounds, provides exciting starting points for talk, painting, sketching, writing, and mathematical investigations. Such an attitude and background experience should open our eyes to the human potential within any environment" (p. 123). Similarly, this book has shown how the kernel design approach provides exciting, starting points for researching, experimenting, and role-playing.

Chapter 1 presented the basic rationale and value of the kernel design as a basis for role-playing and researching. The value of role-playing is summarized by Allen when he states that "drama provides children with an opportunity to discover something of their own personality through exploring that of others in spatial terms, in an imaginative setting. It is an aid to conceptual thinking, and it provides experience in conflict and tension" (p. 231). Frazier (1976) summarized the value of research, discussed at some length in Chapter 1: "Investigative activity remains of prime importance all our lives. Man is a knowledge user. His need for information and ideas sends him seeking help from many sources. Throughout his life experience his skills for collecting knowledge continue to develop as does his power to create information on his own" (p. 93). The diversified roles played by the teacher in

143

this role-playing and researching approach were also discussed.

Chapter 2 provided a framework for the management of the classroom as a stage. Freedom with responsibility was a recurring theme throughout the chapter. Suggestions for interdisciplinary planning and brainstorming investigative, exploratory activities were also presented.

Chapters 3 through 11 exemplified the implementation of the four basic steps for establishing the creative classroom environment as a stage:

Step 1: Synthesizing a narrative statement typifying the area being studied.

Step 2: Researching illustrations depicting the area being studied.

Step 3: Kernelizing the uniqueness of the specific area being studied, using the narrative statement and illustrations as a basis for the kernelization.

Step 4: Drafting of the kernel design and planning related research and role-playing activities.

The examples of kernel designs we have selected are merely illustrative of the approach which can be used with any social studies curriculum. The activities are not exhaustive but rather exemplify some of the divergent exploratory activities possible when interacting with the sample kernel designs.

Chapter 12 outlined the actual physical construction of the kernel designs. Many practical suggestions and illustrations for working with free and/or inexpensive materials were given.

FLEXIBILITY OF THE KERNEL DESIGN

The beauty of the kernel design approach resides in its great flexibility. It spans all age levels and grade levels from kindergarten through junior high school. It has been used as a basis for total integration of the curricula, as well as for a discrete social studies or science unit. Accordingly, the kernel design can consume the entire time of the school day in the informal or open classroom or just a prescribed 30 to 40 minute period for traditional social studies or science. Even when the open classroom approach is not possible or practical, the creative atmosphere of the kernel design remains throughout the day, for several weeks or even longer, as a constant reminder and road map for the development of the discrete social studies topic. Even without planned cross-disciplinary study, the kernels will engender some curricular integration by your class. For example, the tipi and forest kernels for the study of the American Indian community will probably stimulate some pupils to inquire, when studying mathematics, science, or music, how these things were accomplished or enjoyed by the Indians. "Did they have to learn multiplication too?" can lead to some valuable lessons by discovery, lessons relevant to both social studies and mathematics.

The kernel design technique can be used with short-term and long-term projects. One teacher used the pageantry of Mexico and celebrated the numerous fiestas throughout the school year. At the begining of the year, each student was assigned a specific fiesta to research and plan the appropriate celebration.   Since the people make the fiesta what it is - a tradition handed down from one generation to another - both individuals and the whole class researched Mexican culture.   Characteristics of the fiestas that were researched included the rituals of the church, native Indian dances, a sociable market, rodeos, fireworks, and bullfights.

The teacher converted the doorway to the classroom into a kernel which created the illusion of the border between the United States and Mexico. As children entered the classroom each Friday, they were required to know five new Spanish words or phrases in order to get past the border guard. All the furniture and decor of the classroom were labeled with Spanish descriptions. The teacher was amazed by how the Spanish vocabulary of the children (fifth graders) increased. The teacher also painted an outline map of Mexico on the tile floor. As the fiestas were held, villages in which the fiestas originated were painted on the floor. (Water-based latex paints are soluble in ammonia, and clean up off vinyl with relative ease.) Numerous measurement and scaling activities were designed around the floor map. Footsteps with dates and names of events were used to trace the progression of a walk through Mexican history.

THE KERNEL DESIGN: TRIED AND TRUE ·

Since this book describes an innovative approach tried by local teachers, it seems very appropriate to conclude with comments from them.   Richard A. Kohler, administrative coordinator of Discovery School (an individually guided education multiunit school in Mansfield, Ohio) has contributed the following excerpt regarding the experience that he and his three teachers had in implementing the kernel design approach in an economics unit.

Team teaching, interdisciplinary planning, and the multiunit classroom organization with family grouping of children in kindergarten through grade 6 are established goals of Discovery School. The initiation of the kernel design approach definitely enhances these goals and the educational setting already being established.

In preassessing the students' skills in mathematics, a general weakness was identified in the areas of measurement and the use of monetary skills.   The staff suggested a unit of study involving economics as a method of attacking these weaknesses. Through the kernel design approach students would be engaged as much as possible in simulated real-life experiences that involved measurement and currency exchange. The construction of a "city" within the classroom would provide the stage for these role-playing experiences.

The planning time prior to the unit was approximately three weeks. This allowed the staff time to prepare integrated academic lessons and to decide where the building constructions would be located and their approximate sizes. A ground plan of the room was drawn and areas were designated for the respective buildings. Staff members sketched several kernel designs as possible blueprints from which students could select and build their own structures.

The teachers prepared a list of needed materials and a parent 'scrounge committee' was formed to locate the needed items. Latex paints, carpet rolls, large appliance cartons, old sheets, heavy cord, extra-wide masking tape, old paint brushes, and shelfpaper were among the items needed and collected by the scrounge committee. These were the same materials the students "bought" when it came time to construct the city. It was amazing what thrifty buyers they became when they had to spend their own money!

During the second week before the start of the unit, a class meeting was held with the students to discuss the unit, to establish the kinds of businesses to be constructed, and to explain the ground rules of the unit. It was decided that a real estate company and bank were necessary. Each of the four teachers would supervise no more than three companies. In addition to the bank and real estate companies, a newspaper office, theater, restaurant, fix-it shop, post office, sign shop, charm school and beauty shop, construction company, and city government would be established.

Time schedules in the form of either pictorial or written contracts were developed by the teachers. The contracts allowed the students to schedule their time at their 'city job' and at the various related learning stations which were set up for the integrated research activities of the unit.

The week before the unit started, the students made their job selections, formed companies, received a bank book with $50.00 per company (Discovery School currency), purchased the acreage by the square foot, and bought the materials from those collected by the parents to construct their kernel design businesses. Working during recess, before and after school, the students soon converted their schoolroom into a miniature city. One area of the room was designated as the paint and construction zones. Areas outside of the school building were also used for this purpose when weather permitted.

Those simplified elements of each company that best symbolized that business for the children were selected and constructed. For example, the children associated bright colors and an entrance canopy with a restaurant. (See Fig. 13-1.)

In contrast to the bright colors and canopy of the restaurant, the students working in the theater saw the doorway with curtains as symbolic of their business. (See Fig. 13-2.)

Members of the real estate company saw their business as big but with subdued colors, so they constructed a two-story building painted in mute colors. (See Fig. 13-3.)

In the case of the post office, a mail sorting box and large mail box kernelized this business for the children. (See Fig. 13-4.)

The major point to be considered here is that those characteristics which best symbolized the business for the children formed the kernel designs.

The benefits of using the kernel design approach are countless. There was tremendous evidence of creative activity by the children. They grew in their ability to 'see' the relationship of the academic lessons to the real world. The enthusiasm of the children for this unit

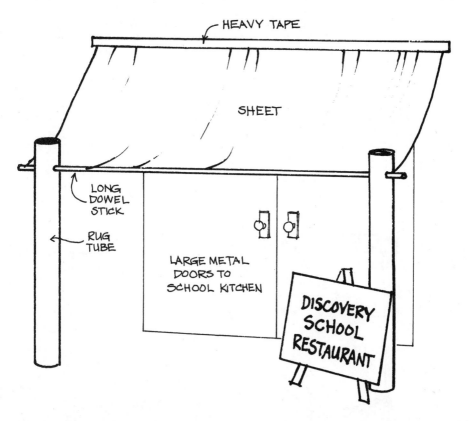

Fig. 13-1   A Kernel Design of a Restaurant   (James Thorpe)

was especially noted by the parents and other educators.   'What
excitement for learning,' said one parent, who herself is a teacher.
'I've never seen anything like it!' When enthusiasm to learn is present
in the classroom environment, the teaching-learning process really
happens.

One of the reasons the enthusiasm of the students reached such a
high pitch lies in the fact that all of the students actually participated
to the fullest. The child with a creative self-directed learning style
obviously found an outlet in this kernel design approach. But most
importantly, the shy, reserved student also became completely
involved, thanks to the role-playing possibilities provided by the kernel
designs. For example, one of the authors of this book was extremely
surprised one day to see a shy kindergarten child shampoo the hair of
one of the teachers at the beauty parlor. What a great opportunity for
child-teacher interaction. One seven-year-old girl who had previously
not been motivated in the area of math volunteered to be the treasurer
of the beauty shop. Her enthusiasm was so great that each night she

asked her father to help balance the books for her company. Her father commented that he had never thought it possible to motivate his child in the area of math. He couldn't believe how eager she was to demonstrate her newly acquired math abilities.

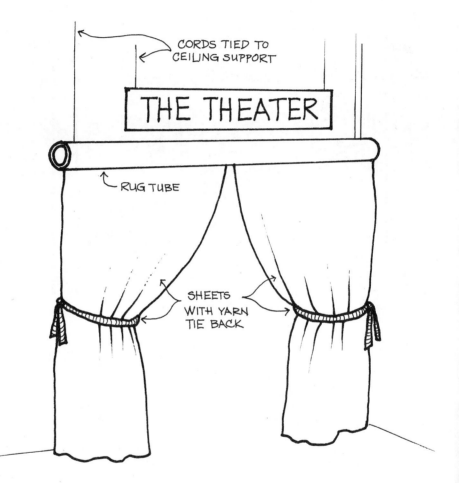

Fig. 13-2   A Kernel Design of a Theater   (James Thorpe)

Although this kernel design in economics started with emphasis on mathematics skills, in actuality it became a completely integrated unit of study. Journals and daily logs kept by the student on the progress of their businesses, reports on field trips, and readings on famous American industrialists served as the sources of many language arts activities.

Discussions on welfare, the impact of economics on the lives of people in different parts of the United States, newspaper clippings on the fading of the aircraft industry, the space program cutback and the plight of the farmers led to mapping, graphing, and numerous chart activities in social studies. One science class, studying structures, even researched and constructed a small

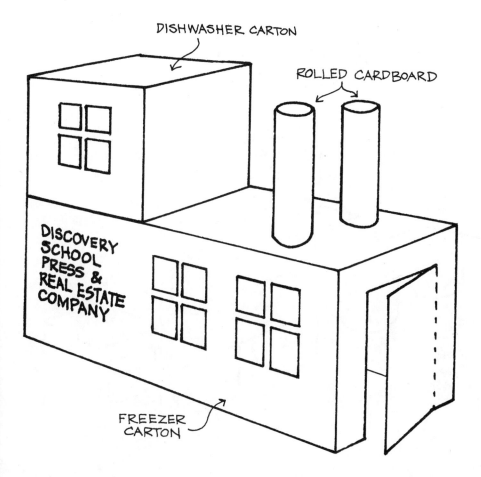

DISHWASHER CARTON

ROLLED CARDBOARD

DISCOVERY
SCHOOL
PRESS &
REAL ESTATE
COMPANY

FREEZER
CARTON

Fig. 13-3   A Kernel Design of a Real Estate Company   (James Thorpe)

wooden bridge over a small creek that runs near the school. (See Fig. 13-5.) And of course, the potential for art activities in any kernel design is obvious.

This highly successful complex unit of study utilizing the kernel design approach was not the first kernel design constructed by the staff of Discovery School.   Units on colonial America, pioneer life, and the <u>Mayflower</u> had preceded it.   It was not easy to plan integrated units of study around those

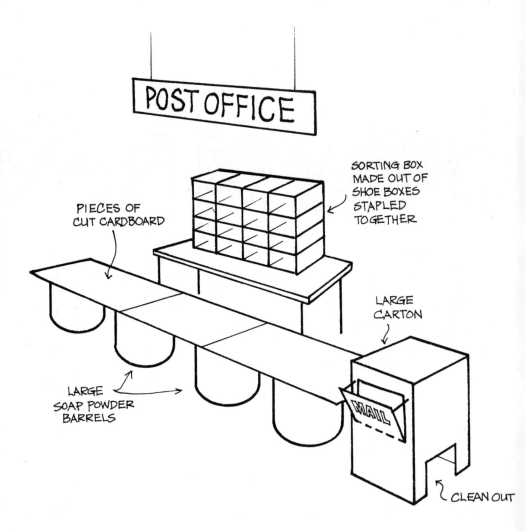

Fig. 13-4 A Kernel Design of a Post Office   (James Thorpe)

initial kernel designs. Teachers and administrators alike were inhibited by
the fear that the kernels might prove to be no more than 'window dressing' in
the classroom and might even distract students from the learning environment. As the students' enthusiasm grew, the teachers' confidence also grew.
The creative adrenalin of the staff really flowed. More elaborate and well-
planned kernel designs and integrated lessons were developed with each
subsequent unit.

The children of Discovery School certainly experienced the philosophy
endorsed by Rogers (1970) that "children should live more fully and more
richly <u>now</u>, rather than at some ill-defined time in the distant future.

Fig. 13-5   Discovery School Bridge: A Kernel Design Activity

Education, then, is not preparation for life; rather education is life with all
its excitement, challenge, and possibilities" (p. 289). Similarly, the
excitement, challenge, and possibilities offered through the kernel design
approach are applauded by other in-service teachers who have used the
approach in their classrooms. A random selection of their responses is
included here:

- "Teaching became a joy for me as I observed children discover the joy of
  learning."

- "The enthusiasm and motivation among the students was dramatically increased."

- "Students love the idea of being researchers."

- "Children learned to work cooperatively rather than competitively."

- "The unmotivated became motivated."

- "I think it's a good way to bring social studies to life for the children."

- "Even my fifth graders enjoyed role-playing."

- "The students became real leaders and organizers during the kernel design unit."

- "The problem of how to motivate students seemed to disappear."

- "I discovered the 'real children' in my class as they became involved in role-playing. I was amazed how I had misjudged the abilities of the children before I used the kernel design approach."

- "The students far surpassed any expectations I had for them. They are much more capable of independent research than I ever trusted them to be."

- "Try it. . . you'll like it!"

- "Initially I resented the graduate course requirement to implement a kernel design because I had inherited a classroom of students with a notoriously bad reputation. I felt my classroom could only result in a greater degree of the already existing chaos. The opposite was true!"

- "The four basic steps to develop a kernel design provide an excellent procedure for lesson planning. The first time I developed a kernel design, I skipped the narrative statement. I realize now this is one of the most important steps. It helps one to recall important, exciting ideas that can often be used as kernel designs."

- "I've always wanted to become a creative teacher. The kernel design approach has helped my dream come true."

- "My kids have learned to work better as a team through the small-group activities provided by the kernel design."

- "One parent called me and asked what happened to her son. She said this was the first time in three years that her son enjoyed going to school."

- "A challenge for both the teacher and the students - a challenge that leads to and fosters growth!"

- "An excellent way to provide vicarious experiences for the students."

- "I never realized how independent and responsible children could be."

- "Students showed a greater self-discipline."

- "Discipline problems diminished as children got involved in activities which they chose."

- "The interest was so great that it was impossible to get the children to go outside for recess."

The remaining chapters of this book, hopefully, will be written in the memories of the children and teachers who accept the challenge of the kernel design approach.   Having achieved the basic goals of the kernel design approach, the lives of the students will better reflect critical thinking and problem-solving skills.   Above all, the approach should better prepare each child to become a positive actor, rather than a passive listener, in life's environment in which "all the world's a stage."

REFERENCES

Allen, J.   "Movement, music, drama, and art."   in Teaching in the British primary school, edited by V.R. Rogers. London: Collier-Macmillan, 1970.

Frazier, A.   Teaching children today: An informal approach.   New York: Harper & Row, 1976.

Marsh, L.   Alongside the child, experiences in the British primary school. New York: Harper & Row, 1970.

Rogers, V.R., ed. Teaching in the British primary school. London: Collier-Macmillan, 1970.

Index

About the Authors

SHIRLEY F. HECK (Ph.D., The University of Wisconsin) is Associate Professor of Early & Middle Childhood Education at The Ohio State University. She is also involved in a number of research and development programs, is Professor of a School Based Integrated Preservice/In-service Elementary Teacher Education program, has served as a selected Team Member of the National Council for the Accreditation of Teacher Education Programs, and as National Consultant for The University of Wisconsin's Developing Mathematical Processes Program. Dr. Heck has had many articles published in professional journals and has contributed several chapters to the book, Explorations into Teaching.

JON P. COBES received his Ph.D. in theater arts from The Ohio State University, his M.A. in Speech, his B.S. in Music Education and a Master's Degree in Library Science. He also studied music at the Mozarteum in Salzburg, Austria. Dr. Cobes is Associate Professor of Library Administration and Director of Learning Resources at The Ohio State University and has written numerous articles for professional journals.